Social Media Marketing In A Week

Nick Smith

I'd like to humbly dedicate this book to the memories of my grandparents, Tony Weston and Andy Whitfield, who all taught me to 'Be Here Now'.

Nick Smith runs a successful online marketing consultancy advising companies how to increase sales and profits using the power of the Internet and by leveraging forgotten assets hidden in their business. As one of the leading direct response marketing consultants in the UK, Nick devises effective traffic strategies using a combination of paid marketing sources, search engine optimization and social media marketing.

Nick is also the author of Successful SEO and Search Marketing in this series of 'In A Week' business books. Visit his website at http://NickTheGeek.com.

Social Media Marketing

Teach Yourself®

Nick Smith

www.inaweek.co.uk

Contents

Introduction

Welcome to the 'Teach Yourself Social Media Marketing in a Week' training course. It is, as the title suggests, a way for you to learn how to do social media marketing in only seven days.

My goal is to teach you everything you need to start, as well as guidance on avoiding the minefield of social media so your first jaunt into the woods does not end in you losing an arm or leg in the process.

I will use all of my wit, charm and sense of humour (such as it is!) to communicate this to you so hopefully it will never be dull. I know what it's like to read a boring, dry textbook and that's the last thing I want for you.

I want to make learning fun, or at the very least not make you fall asleep while you're reading it.

Who is this book for?

If you are new to the world of social media, then this is **the** book for you. If you are more of a jaded professional, this book is not so much for you, though there are some pretty cool marketing tips here that you might not find in other places.

I particularly geared this book for you, the social media newbie, because I know it can be a scary experience when there is just so much to learn. I mean, Facebook is the biggest website in the world. Where do you begin?

That's where I and this book come in. Not only will I show you how to get started with social media but I will also give you the ability and best practices to guide your interactions with your fans and subscribers pretty much forever, even if I can't advise directly on your exact situation or sector you are part of.

In the coming weeks, months and years you'll constantly be assaulted by self-appointed 'social media gurus' telling you about the latest software or course, but in this book I will teach you the principles that will let you know if that latest gadget is a good idea or not.

To paraphrase the famous quote: 'Gimmicks are fleeting but principles are forever.'

I hope you decide to enter the training and get started today because social media is just getting too big to ignore.

In fact, according to one survey, 70 per cent of small businesses interviewed said they were active on Facebook and if you are not one of them, you will be left behind. Every day you put it off makes it that much harder to catch up with them!

Don't get left behind. Get started right now on your way to your social media success.

Nick Smith

SUNDAY

Introduction to social media

Welcome to the beginning of your training. Grab a cup of your favourite beverage as we're heading off into the wilderness that is social media.

This wild world can get a little tangled and well a bit crazy really, but don't panic, I'll hopefully clear up any confusion.

SUNDAY

MONDAY

TUESDAY

WEDNESDAY

THURSDAY

FRIDAY

SATURDAY

What is social media?

Before embarking on our trip to understand social media marketing, it's important we first establish what social media is. Let's face it, social media is a term that is thrown around a lot and everyone is talking about how important it is for businesses.

If Facebook is a social media site and Twitter is a social media site and YouTube is a social media site, doesn't that make pretty much everything on the Internet a social media site?

Not really. Let me explain...

The best way to define what social media is exactly is to break it down. Any method that is used to broadcast to the masses (i.e. the population at large) is considered media. Think newspapers, magazines, TV and radio. If we add to that 'social' then we understand that social media is simply a method of social communications.

This means that social media isn't just a form of media that provides you with information: it also lets you interact with the information, while at the same time providing you with that information.

The interaction can be simple or complex ranging from liking a status on Facebook, leaving a comment on a blog or voting for a video on YouTube, to something more complex like viewing content recommended to you based on your Facebook interests or what your friends on social media have watched recently.

Social media simplified

A good way to think about it is this. Traditional media is a one-way street. They (the media moguls) produce the content and then you can read, watch or listen to it but your ability to provide feedback on the subject is very limited (unless you really have time to write or make a phone call).

Social media, on the other hand, is a two way-street, where the users (be they a business or an individual) can also create the content while they all interact together (not just by providing comments but also by creating videos, taking pictures and more).

This is where the real power of social media is for a business: getting others to create your content or advertisements for you (more on this later).

Social networking, social news, social bookmarking

A source of major confusion for people who are just starting out in social media marketing is thinking that sites such as Facebook or LinkedIn are all that social media is, or, they think that social networking, i.e. Facebook, is all there is to social media.

Social networking is just a part of social media, though it is a massive part. Social networking allows you to connect with fellow industry insiders, co-workers, clients and customers and to build a relationship with your target audience. Social networking sites include Facebook, LinkedIn, Friendster and MySpace.

Social 'news' is not the same as social 'media'. Social news is rather a tool of social media (which is the umbrella term so to speak). This will be talked about at length later. A few samples of social news sites include:

- Reddit
- Digg
- Propeller
- Gather

Social bookmarking is also a tool of social media. This is a tool that allows people to tag websites and search through websites that others have tagged. A few social bookmarking sites include:

- Diigo
- Folkd
- Delicious (formerly http://del.icio.us now http://www.delicious.com)

Other social sites are used to share music, videos and images, such as:

- Flickr
- YouTube
- Pinterest

There are 'Wiki' sites that also allow interaction (all started by Wikipedia) where readers submit the content and interact on that content through edits. (The TARDIS Index File is my favourite. Yes, I am a Doctor Who geek and proud of it!)

What is social media marketing?

Now we come to the core: social media marketing. In its broadest sense social media marketing is a form of marketing that entrepreneurs and companies can use to establish, maintain and expand an online presence and reputation. The key to social media marketing is to build a relationship with your target audience.

This is where many businesses go 'off-piste'. They make the mistake in thinking that social media is a place to sell their product or service. Social media marketing is a process and the very first step in social media marketing is creating engaging and informative content that readers will want to share with their circle of friends, i.e. their social network.

The content that you create (your message) will spread as your target audience shares it. That content needs to present you as an authority in your field so that it establishes trust. A reader will share the content you create if it is informative, well written and gives them something of value. That one reader will then share it with everyone they know and those people will share with their friends and on and on. This is what's meant when you hear something goes 'viral'.

In the dinosaur days before the Internet, this was known as word-of-mouth marketing. Word-of-mouth marketing is still one of, if not the, most powerful forms of marketing out there and it is what social marketing is geared around and what makes it tick.

This is because people always trust their family and friends more than they trust an organization. After all if your best friend recommends that you go and see a specific film you are more likely to go to watch it because your friend gains nothing out of referring you and they know what you like. The weight of their word and knowledge of you is greater than a paid actor on an advertisement.

Social media marketing tools

It is fair to say that social media marketing has been around as long as the Internet. Any time information is shared there is almost always word-of-mouth action that accompanies it although, in the past, it was more likely to be done using email and discussion forums.

As of 2012 there is a vast array of social media outlets available to companies to help them 'spread the word'. Here is a brief list of some of the most popular social media marketing websites today:

- Facebook
- Twitter
- LinkedIn
- Google+
- YouTube
- Delicious
- Flickr
- Pinterest

Collectively, they represent billions of connections globally. Facebook has over a billion users and Twitter's network delivers 350 million tweets a day from its 140 million users. YouTube has 72 hours of video uploaded to it every minute and 800 million unique hits every month.

Another mistake that is commonly made with social media is to believe that all social media sites are ideal for everything. The key to effective social media marketing is going to the sites that your target audience frequents. There are dozens if not hundreds of social networking sites for specific niches and markets. Facebook is not the be-all and end-all, and it isn't always the best option for your marketing efforts.

Along with the various sites out there, there are numerous methods that entrepreneurs and businesses can use. Later in the book we will go into greater detail on the tools you can use for social media marketing but here is just a small sample:

- Blogging
- Copywriting
- Social networking

- Podcasting
- Videos
- Bookmarking
- Reputation management

Why you need to care about social media marketing

The Internet has made customers (potential, current and future) educated consumers. People now have access to businesses, products and services from all over the world. You are no longer just competing with the business down the street. Today, depending on your product/service, you may need to beat the world. Social media marketing is one of the main tools for that.

If you are a company who just markets and services in your local area, you should still use social media marketing but you don't need to beat the world, just the marketing efforts of the guy down the street.

Think about all the time you spend on your favourite social networking site, or the blog posts you read and comment on. You are probably doing it from a personal perspective every day. Now all you have to do is think about it and take action from a business perspective.

What is it about that blog or Facebook page that you liked that makes them stand out? Why did you reach out and interact?

From a business perspective social media marketing will allow you to become a social business. This means courting your prospects through the entire process of buying your product or service. We are talking about total customer care. While the Internet has made business overall less personal because you have the ability to reach customers worldwide, social media marketing offers you the opportunity to connect with your prospects on a personal level. You don't have to bring them into your store. You can reach them where they are at times that are convenient to them.

Social media marketing can also be used to grow your business. Where else do you have instant access to your target audience for free? Pay attention to what they are talking about and what their needs are as this opens doorways to new products and services. Perhaps you have an idea for something new already? Your followers on social media are your test market or unofficial focus group.

The question really shouldn't be 'Why should you care about social media marketing?' rather, 'Why aren't you actively pursuing and using social media to its fullest extent?'

Still not sold on the idea?

Here is a list of ten reasons why social media is the key to building and growing a profitable business.

1 Social media is the No. 1 of all online activities, surpassing email, porn and even fantasy football and baseball.
2 More than 60 per cent of people on the Internet visit social networking websites daily.
3 The average budget spent on company blogs and social media has tripled in three years which means your competition are getting ready to steal your lunch!
4 Up to 57 per cent of companies have acquired a customer via a blog, 62 per cent via LinkedIn, 52 per cent via Facebook and 44 per cent via Twitter.
5 A huge 74 per cent of consumers rely on social networks to guide purchasing decisions.
6 Facebook has over a billion users (if it were a country, it would be the third largest in the world), with half of them checking in every day.
7 As of 1 July 2012, Twitter had 140 million active accounts sending 350 million tweets a day.
8 The Google+1 button is used **5 billion** (yes, that's billion with a 'b') times a day.
9 Pinterest is driving more referral traffic to websites than YouTube, Google+ and LinkedIn combined.
10 And the number one reason is... access to, and marketing with, social media is predominantly free.

Social media marketing done the right way

As with most things, there is a right way and a wrong way to use social media marketing. There are a few very common mistakes that marketers make in the social media world, and there are a few best practices that you need to know about before we go through the rest of the week.

- **Make the right first impression:** it is far easier to take your time and make the right first impression than to spend time fixing the wrong one. Remember the basis of this type of marketing is word of mouth. It only takes one dissatisfied or unimpressed customer to ruin an entire marketing plan. One blogger managed to shut down an entire new product line at lingerie store Victoria's Secret when she offered her opinion that a certain new piece on sale was 'overt racism masked behind claims of inspired fashion'.
- **Have a unified marketing message:** social media marketing should not be seen as something separate from the rest of your marketing. It is an integral part of your marketing plan. Every marketing tool you use should drive your business towards the same goal. Yes, you can use social media marketing for branding, but don't stop there. Don't let that be all you are using social media for.
- **Social media marketing strategy:** don't make the mistake in thinking that you have to use every social media marketing tool out there. Likewise, don't use the tools without having a strategy to what you are doing. If you are creating a Facebook group, are you also engaging people in forums and are you creating informative content for sites like YouTube? What is the aim of the social media tools you are using? Are you just trying to get out there? Do you want to introduce a new product? Bottom line? Know exactly why you're doing social media marketing.
- **Know where your audience is:** there are hundreds and thousands of social media sites out there, all of which have a different audience and serve a different purpose. Go to the sites that your target audience populates. Take the time

to do the research to find out where they are. Facebook isn't the only answer, and it isn't the right answer for everybody.

- **Engage your audience:** do not sell through social media. Social media marketing is about building your reputation, building relationships with your customers and giving them information they can use. If you have a Facebook page, that is **not** where you sell your services. You post content that provides value and directs them to another source of good content that will direct them to a capture page (where you can get names, emails and so on) and *then* you sell to them. Selling is never the first part of any effective social media marketing plan.

- **Sharing too often:** just as there is email spam, there is social media spam. When you post too often on social networking sites people tend to stop paying attention to what you are saying. It isn't that if you have ten excellent tips to help your customers or clients that you can't post them, but it is better to schedule those posts to come out perhaps two a day over a week. Remember you want people to pay attention to what you have to say, not roll their eyes and click right past your post.

- **Avoid self-proclaimed social media experts:** OK, so I get the irony of this point since you're learning how to become an expert with social media by reading a book written by a social media expert. The bottom line is this. With hundreds or thousands of different social media sites out there, it's impossible for any one person (even me) to be an expert at all of them. Can they specialize in a few? Absolutely! Can they be an expert at one? Absolutely! Is there a be-all and end-all social media guru out there? Unlikely!

- **Reputation management:** building a strong, well-liked brand using social media marketing can do much more than help sell your products or services. Strong brands with a loyal following cultivated by engaging your followers can help you bounce back from any negative comments or reviews your company has received. It's one of the reasons why global brands like Toyota and US brands like Martha Stewart have bounced back from some really awful press.

If you're new to social media marketing it's best to start out with just one outlet used most by your customers. You need to make sure the outlet is appropriate for your business as well. If you offer a service for professionals, social networking sites like LinkedIn are better suited for business. Once you become familiar with how social media works, you can start repurposing your content to other outlets.

Building a strong brand founded on deep-seated relationships is the name of the game. Listen to your customers' needs, wants and concerns, and respond to them accordingly. They have to trust you and be willing to back you up should something arise that challenges your good standing. The thing is, people are ten times more likely to buy your offerings if they have faith and trust in you. They will also be the first ones to have your back covered when any negativity comes around.

After you get the hang of using social media marketing, it becomes easier and easier to manage your reputation. Not only that but it gets easier, and more fun.

Summary

Today you learned that social media is not the web as whole but a media conversation platform that goes both ways from producers to consumers and vice versa. Social media also does not only equal Facebook. While Facebook is a big part of social media there are really hundreds of social sites that all have their uses and particular aims.

You also discovered that there are three forms of social media: social networking sites like Facebook, social news sites like Reddit, social bookmarking sites like Diigo, and other huge social sites that have other specialties that are very useful like YouTube, Flickr, and Pinterest.

One thing that is worth repeating is that the key to social media is not to sell but to build a relationship with your customers. Do not miss this, and say this every time you wake up when you first look in the mirror: 'I will not be salesy on my social pages...' (OK, maybe you don't have to do that, but you get the point).

I then showed you how much you need to be on social media (many of your competitors are already there), plus the fact that it is mostly free! Then we went through a checklist of seven things you need to do social media the right way (these warrant repeat reading, so be sure to bookmark that page and highlight the ones that you will need the most).

Fact-check (answers at the back)

Ten questions to help you remember what you learned more clearly:

1. Social sites are:
   a) Facebook, because it is the only social website ☐
   b) Social sites are where users provide feedback on the experience ☐
   c) Social sites are where users create the content for the site ☐
   d) Both B and C are correct ✔

2. Traditional media:
   a) Is a powerhouse of interactivity with fun stuff around every corner ☐
   b) As stale as month old bread and trying to catch up ✔
   c) Is boring ☐
   d) Both B and C are correct ☐

3. Something going 'viral' means:
   a) Lots of people are sharing and interacting with the content you produced ✔
   b) You need to hide inside and don't shake anyone's hand ☐
   c) You also need to get a vaccine ☐
   d) A marketing campaign aimed at healthcare ☐

4. Social media is:
   a) The number 2 destination of all traffic online ☐
   b) The number 1 destination of all traffic online ✔
   c) The number 3 destination of all traffic online ☐
   d) Not very important ☐

5. You need to be on social media because:
   a) Your customers are there talking about you. ☐
   b) Your potential customers are there ☐
   c) It's just what everyone else does ☐
   d) Both A and B are right ✔

6. Social media costs:
   a) Tons of cash ☐
   b) Lots of dough ☐
   c) Is mostly free to get started (though it costs time) ✔
   d) Many moolah ☐

7. You need to be very careful:
   a) To make the right impression ☐
   b) To engage your audience ☐
   c) Not to share too often ☐
   d) All of the above ✔

8. If you have very bad press:
   a) With a good running social campaign anything is possible ✔
   b) You will never be able to get back to where you were, go back to your day job ☐
   c) It is tough but doable to get back to where you were ✔ ✗
   d) Ignore it ☐

9. The name of the game is:
   a) A strong brand built on deep-seated relationships ✔
   b) Monopoly ☐
   c) Being really good and never messing up ☐
   d) Getting people to buy bunches of stuff ☐

10. People are more likely to buy from you:

a) When you make them a good offer ❑

b) When you make them the same offer over and over again ❑

c) When they like and trust you ☑

d) When they are amazed by your special sales copy ❑

SUNDAY

MONDAY

TUESDAY

WEDNESDAY

THURSDAY

FRIDAY

SATURDAY

MONDAY

Successful case studies

Quick recap

Here we are on day two of your week to social media marketing success.

Hopefully you are still with me, because today we get a little breather. On day one we went over what social media was and the different tools that make up social media marketing. Keep these various tools in mind as we move forward. We will be talking more about creating a social media marketing plan and different strategies that you can use, and this will be important as you answer the questions to figure out what tools will work best for you.

The goal for today is to reveal to you the potential that social media marketing has for your business when it is done well. We are going to peruse a few case studies and discuss why you can't focus on the return on investment (ROI) of social media marketing right away.

Case studies

It is rather incredible that with the relatively short history of social media marketing in the online world that companies, both large and small, have found great success using social networking platforms to enhance their brand, boost business and provide customer service. A couple of the most successful social media marketing campaigns have involved the creative use of social networking sites such as Twitter and Facebook.

Fiesta Movement by Ford

Probably one of the very first and most successful social media campaigns was launched by Ford in April 2009. It was called the Fiesta Movement. The tactic that Ford used was very innovative and sort of cool. What they did was to loan a Ford Fiesta to 100 of the top bloggers to use for six months. In exchange, all that Ford asked of the bloggers was to upload a video to YouTube about the Fiesta and post an independent account of their experience with the car on their respective blogs. (Why I couldn't have been one of those bloggers I will never know. Oh well, maybe next time.)

The campaign was a massive success. There were more than 700 videos created by the bloggers, which generated over 6 million views on YouTube (this is a major amount as the average video only gets 100 views), more than 3 million Twitter impressions and Flickr was flooded with more than 670,000 photos of the Ford Fiesta. There was so much buzz created about this vehicle that 50,000 consumers in the United States alone wanted more information about the Ford Fiesta and a whopping 90 per cent of them had never owned a Ford before.

In the first six days, Ford sold 10,000 Ford Fiestas (meaning they made millions...).

Ford didn't stop there. The success drove Ford (pun completely intended!) to look even closer at social media. They went looking for actual feedback from consumers. They went to sites such as http://www.SyncMyRide.com (a forum site where owners of cars talk to one another), which had logged a number of complaints about the automated voice on the Ford SYNC system. This information helped Ford make improvements to the quality of the voice.

So all in all, Ford used forums, Flickr, YouTube and blogs to implement an incredibly successful social media marketing campaign.

Clorox

Clorox took social media and tweaked it to create incredible revenue and optimal awareness. What they did was host a Green Works Webpage in 2010. They targeted women between the ages of 25 and 34. The goal of the social media marketing campaign was to increase awareness of Green Works, products that are environmentally friendly. The tool that Clorox decided to use was Facebook, targeting users that had listed 'green' and 'clean' on their profiles.

A Nielsen follow-up study done after the campaign showed that the 'intent to purchase' the Green Works detergent went up by seven per cent among Facebook users. The follow-up study also showed that there was a whopping 12 per cent increase in brand awareness. (These are pretty big figures for such big brands with massive awareness already.)

Budweiser

During the FIFA World Cup soccer tournament in South Africa in 2010, Budweiser launched one of the most successful Facebook campaigns to date. Their campaign was called 'Bud United: Show Your True Colors'.

All the campaign did was make it so that followers could paint their faces on their Facebook profile with their favourite team's colours. This endeavour generated an incredible level of engagement with followers, with more than 2.5 million people opting to paint their faces.

Almost 1 million people 'liked' the Bud United Page by the end of the campaign. This is one of the most classic examples of how a company can generate engagement with their target audience using social media and get the users to create your ads and content for you.

So what about the little guy?

I know, you're sitting there thinking that the big boys can do social media marketing successfully for sure. After all they have the manpower and the money to back their efforts. So let's take a look at a few small companies and how they used social media marketing the right way. Also remember, in general, social media marketing is a free exercise.

Gonuts with Donuts

Gonuts with Donuts is a small company based in Sri Lanka that successfully created an advertising campaign on Facebook. This was so successful they now have more than 10,000 followers (most companies barely crack a few hundred) to whom they post updates on Facebook on a regular basis but they have increased their sales volume so much that they have been able to open up several additional stores.

Triumvirate Environmental

Triumvirate Environmental is in business to help clients make sure that the work environment is as safe as possible. They make sure that their clients are compliant with all safety standards. Furthermore they help clients create solutions for disposing of hazardous waste, as well as assisting with other environmental programmes.

They started doing online marketing in 2006 using Google AdWords. At first their marketing was lacklustre but once they started focusing on inbound social media marketing to support their lead generation techniques things started taking off.

The result? Over $1 million in revenue that they directly attributed to social media marketing by using search engine optimization, blogging and the business social network LinkedIn. Today they use a combination of social media tools to increase revenue and brand awareness that includes blogging, Facebook, Twitter, LinkedIn and other online marketing tools. Not bad for free!

AJ Bombers

AJ Bombers is an even smaller company, located in Wisconsin and employing 20 people. What's impressive about their social media marketing endeavour is that they are a pioneer in the industry.

Joe Sorge, the owner of AJ Bombers, will be the first to admit that the key to social media marketing is to first have a great product. Sorge believes that is what he has. Simply put, the best burger in town.

The first part of their social media marketing started with Twitter. They have an incredible 4,000+ followers. Bombers used Twitter to not only let people know about his new restaurant but also to track what people were saying about it and adjusting as they went.

They also started to utilize Foursquare (which allows users to log in and tag places that they have visited) and they combined that with clever promotional events. In this game AJ Bombers partnered with another local company that sold boats. It ended up becoming a fun and interactive game for his social visitors that generated more customers coming into both AJ Bombers and the other retailer.

What it all means

Social media marketing offers an avenue for small businesses to compete with the 'big dogs' and, when properly used, can give your company extra business on a large or small scale. Remember though that you aren't always going to see a huge return on your social media marketing efforts at first. Word-of-mouth marketing can take some time, and takes effort on your part like anything else.

Here are a few traits that all successful social media marketing campaigns run by small businesses have in common:

- They all commit weekly resources that are used to create content and engage customers in social media.
- They all use a method that's able to provide insight into how social media marketing is affecting their business so they are able to establish what is working and what isn't.
- They all regularly use a combination of platforms such as Twitter, blogs, Facebook, LinkedIn and other tools to create content.

- They **don't** use every social platform out there; they invest their time in the platforms that their target audience uses and have the best ROI.
- They all use social media to generate traffic to events that are offline as well as online.
- They all establish very clear expectations for their customers as to the frequency and types of social media interactions that their company is willing to provide.
- They all use social media to establish their company as a thought leader in the industry. Be a pioneer!
- They all make sure to use clear calls to action and opportunities to create leads and acquire new customers through social media.
- They don't just put stuff on social media, they also pay attention to what is out there. They read what people are saying about them and their competition and use that to improve what they are doing.
- They all keep a balance between organic and paid search engine traffic.

Hopefully by now you can see a little bit of the impact that social media marketing can have on your business.

If a small burger joint in Wisconsin can use it to generate thousands and thousands of followers and into joint ventures with other local businesses then the possibilities are endless for your business as well.

Now tomorrow we are going to look at how to get started with social media marketing and I really can't wait to show it to you. Make sure you have paper and a pen to take some notes while going through the next chapter because I am going to be walking your company step by step through the process of creating a truly 'kick-****' social media marketing campaign.

Until then, have a great rest of your day!

Summary

Today we focused on some case studies, both big and small. We looked at Ford with their blogger outreach that ended in massive sales, Budweiser's campaign that ended in tons and tons of interaction and fans, and Clorox who experienced a huge jump in brand awareness simply through a Facebook like campaign.

For the little guys we saw that even a place in the wilderness of Sri Lanka can find customers and drive business through social media, and that creating games with Foursquare and combining it with different business partners can be a good way to success.

We also learned that focusing on social platforms that matter for your business like the company that focused on business-to-business relationships on LinkedIn that produced huge revenue.

Most of all, I shared with you the main things that businesses that succeed in breaking through in social media have in common, which can pretty much be summed up in this

SUNDAY
MONDAY
TUESDAY
WEDNESDAY
THURSDAY
FRIDAY
SATURDAY

statement: they are balanced, pioneering companies that focus on the bottom line in all they do, and because of this they pay attention to what is working, what isn't, and pay attention to each and every customer complaint and compliment.

Fact-check (answers at the back)

Ten questions for your grey matter to help you remember today:

1. The Ford Motor Company gave Fiestas to:
   a) Other companies ❏
   b) Groups of random people ❏
   c) Bloggers ■
   d) Your neighbour ❏

2. A key part of Ford's marketing was:
   a) YouTube ❏
   b) Twitter ❏
   c) Flickr ❏
   d) All of the above ■

3. Budweiser asked one simple thing during its world cup campaign:
   a) Dress special ❏
   b) Paint your face your team colours ■
   c) Get a temporary tattoo ❏
   d) Give them money ❏

4. Social media is only for the company 'giants' out there:
   a) True ❏
   b) False ■

5. Go Nuts With Donuts does at least this one thing to create buzz:
   a) Special promotion posting ■
   b) Posting pictures ❏
   c) Posting videos ❏
   d) Coming up with clever questions ❏

6. Triumvirate Environmental probably initially found success on LinkedIn:
   a) Because that social site is better then Facebook ❏
   b) LinkedIn caters to businesses (which is Triumvirate Environmental's target market) ■
   c) Triumvirate Environmental got lucky ❏
   d) We can't really be sure ❏

7. AJ Bombers found success on:
   a) Twitter ❏
   b) Foursquare ❏
   c) Facebook ❏
   d) A and B ■

8. Foursquare is a good site for:
   a) Multinational corporations ❏
   b) People to say hi to friends ❏
   c) Only businesses ❏
   d) People to find local businesses and local businesses to be found ■

9. You should:
   a) Try every social site and hope you find the best ❏
   b) Research to figure out which social site is best for you ■
   c) Ask your geeky friend which is the best site for you ❏
   d) Guess which are the best sites for you ❏

10. You should always:

a) Commit weekly resources to social sites ☐

b) Be working to get new leads ☐

c) Interacting with your customers ☐

d) Do all of the above ☐

SUNDAY

MONDAY

TUESDAY

WEDNESDAY

THURSDAY

FRIDAY

SATURDAY

TUESDAY

Getting started with social media marketing

Quick recap

Welcome to Tuesday!

Now it is time for us to get into the real meat and potatoes of social media marketing. Let's recap what you have learned so far:

- Social media is any media platform where the users create the content with high levels of interactivity such as Facebook, Wikipedia, Flickr and YouTube.
- Social networking is only one tool of social media, not the whole enchilada.
- Social media marketing is using various social media tools to build your online reputation and create solid relationships with your target audience.
- That there is a right way and a wrong way to do social media marketing.
- Social media marketing is really just good-old-fashioned word-of-mouth marketing that we all know and love taken to a huge level because of the size of the audience.
- It is free for the most part and very powerful.
- That when a company does social media marketing the right way the ROI is incomparable.

Take a moment and get out a piece of paper and a pen. Today we are going to go through the steps to setting up your social media marketing plan and I'm going to steer as far away from 'corporate-speak' as I possibly can. Plain English will do the job fine for us here.

Creating your social media marketing plan

By the end of this exercise, you should aim to have your entire marketing plan in front of you.

Remember social media marketing can't be a separate entity from the rest of your marketing. It all needs to work together towards the same goal. Marketing plans are frequently adjusted to meet a current need so that you are looking at creating a social media aspect to your overall plan. What is the goal of your current marketing plan?

So, ask yourself these questions:

- Is my current marketing plan bringing me closer to my desired goals?
- In what ways can social media further my marketing efforts?
- What do I want to achieve with social media marketing?
- Who am I trying to reach?
- Do I know where they are on the web?

Take a few moments to answer those questions. Your answers don't have to be exact and there isn't really a right or wrong answer. Asking those five questions is really just to get you going and thinking.

You see, before you can go forward you have to have an idea of where you are now.

This is where the paper and pen are going to come in handy because we are going to walk through a ten-step process for laying the foundation of your social media marketing plan.

Ten-step process for creating a social media marketing plan

1. Determine your goals

Determining the goals of any marketing endeavour is vital to the success of those efforts so don't go past this point till you have got this nailed. If you don't know why you are doing something, you aren't going to be motivated to do it correctly and eventually (sooner rather than later) you are going to stop doing it.

It's like kicking a ball in the middle of a football pitch in a championship game and not knowing the idea was to get to the end of the field and kick the ball into the goal! You would just kick the ball for a bit, get the snot knocked out of you by the other pros, and you'd probably end up running home to your parents or going and do something else more fun.

So answer these questions:

- What do you want to get out of your social media marketing efforts? More customers/leads? If so how many?
- Do you want greater brand awareness? If so, you need to clarify exactly what this means.
- Do you want more visitors to a website?
- Why exactly are you doing social media marketing?

Here are a few possible answers to get you started:

- To generate direct sales
- Offering it as a form of customer service
- Reputation building
- To build customer loyalty
- Company/product/service launch
- Company/product/service re-launch

The goals are really endless. The key is to determine what your goals are and to make them doable and measurable. Write them down now and let's move to the next step so that we can work through creating the foundation of your social media marketing plan.

2. Evaluate resources

This is important to determine and define. Why? Social media requires interaction, and if you are going to use social networking as one of the tools you need to know who is going to maintain that and where the content that is going to be used is coming from. This is your online reputation we are talking about: don't pass this step by saying 'I'll figure it out later'. That just won't do!

So now answer these questions to the best of your ability:

- Who is going to create the social media content? (Blogs, articles, videos, images, status updates, etc.)
- Who will maintain the social media accounts?
- Who will be the voice(s) of your business, the one responding to questions on your company's behalf?
- Do you have the in-house technical ability to be a part of online conversation? If you answer no, are you or a member of staff willing to learn or are you able to outsource?
- Can you, or someone you have on your team, write well?

Knowing if you have the right people in place is vital. Without the right people your social media marketing will fail, regardless of how incredible your plan is. If you don't currently have these key people you need to look at how you will acquire them. We will go over that later.

3. Know your audience

We are going to assume for the moment that you know who your audience is. You may have already spent the time needed to establish the demographic you are going after based on the products or services you offer. When it comes to social media marketing, understanding your audience is really what you need to do.

You need to understand where your target market is online. This isn't the same as your demographic or running an ad in the paper or putting a billboard up somewhere to catch the attention of everyone, including your market. No, social media marketing is about getting to know your market on an intimate level.

This is where a little research needs to be done. You have to determine the places they frequent online. Everyone almost always assumes that Facebook is the first place or, worse, the only place to go. Yes, Facebook is great and I would agree that it should be a part of most social media marketing plans but it is only a part.

From a social networking point of view there are hundreds if not thousands of social networks out there. Wikipedia has a partial list of some of them and who they cater to. See http://en.wikipedia.org/wiki/List_of_social_networking_websites for more details.

This is just a small sample of the social networks. Just skimming through the list you can see each social network has their own audience, and this is why Facebook can't be the only social network your business uses. Just because a sector or niche-specific social network may 'only' have members in the hundreds or thousands, it doesn't mean you should ignore it. These will be laser-targeted potential customers and clients.

Beyond the social networks, are there particular forums or online communities that your audience frequents? Where do they get the information they need to solve a problem they have? Take the time and find out because those are the places you want to be; if it helps, think about what your audience would type in a search like '[your sector] forum' or '[your niche] blog'.

Once you have established where your audience is you can figure out what type of information they want from you. You will get to know their likes and dislikes. I cannot stress enough that social media marketing is really about getting to know your market and catering to their needs. The selling comes later.

Now when you create content you aren't selling to them, not directly anyway. You are providing a service to them, engaging them, finding out their exact needs and building a relationship based on trust and respect. You are giving them a reason to buy from/work with you and not your competitor.

4. Create amazing content

Don't treat your audience as if they are not as smart as you. Once you have figured out where they are online, and you have spent time finding out what they want, take the time to create content that gives them what they want and makes them feel special and smart for finding you.

If you notice that your audience prefers videos or images and that's what really gets them excited and talking, it really wouldn't make much sense just creating a plain ol' blog post.

This isn't about reinventing the wheel. This is about making the wheel you are offering better than everyone else's out there, so check out what is working with the other wheel makers and do it better or different (in a good way).

5. Marketing effort integration

All of your social media marketing efforts need to work together. This means that they need to feed off one another. Cross-promote your social media accounts to your audience. If your audience is on a social network, there are a few blogs that they frequent and they like video, then you need to make sure you let them know that they can find more great content on your blog with integrated YouTube videos and on playlists on your YouTube Channel by promoting this on your social network page.

Your social media marketing and the traditional marketing you are doing **also** need to work together. You need to be promoting your online endeavours on your brochures, advertisements, radio, etc. These marketing efforts should all be working towards the same goal and they should all be working together to support one another. This is marketing synergy at its core.

6. Create a schedule

If you are an entrepreneur starting and running your own business and your employees consist of, well, just you and your dog, creating an effective schedule is very important. It is very easy to spend more time than is actually needed on a social network. If you are using multiple social media platforms you want to make sure that you are allocating enough time in your day to use them effectively.

Getting sucked into emails and social networks are two of the biggest productivity killers that a businessperson or employee can get caught up with; honestly, from a marketing perspective, you don't need more than 20 minutes on a social network. So create a schedule: spend five minutes on Twitter before checking your email, then pop onto the social network. You will want to repeat the same thing at the end of the day before you close up shop. Twitter, email and networks.

7. The 80/20 rule

This is important. We have stressed that social media isn't really about you, it's about your audience. We have also mentioned that social media isn't really where you sell your product or service right off the bat. So when you are online using your various social media tools, keep in mind that 80 per cent of your time should be spent on activities that are not self-promoting and really no more than 20 per cent should be spent on self-promotion. Social media marketing is about helping your customers/clients.

8. Quality over quantity

This is twofold. It is far better to post content that is useful to your customer be it only once a day or a couple of times a week than to flood them with useless crud (to put it nicely). It is also better to have 1,000 loyal engaged followers than to have 10,000 followers that sign up to get something and then never interact with you again.

Quality goes a lot further than quantity. Less is most definitely more.

9. Control

It is your audience that will dictate the flow of any online conversation. The reason that you want them to do this is that you want your audience to feel as if the conversation is theirs. When someone is able to take ownership, and make something theirs, they develop an emotional connection to whatever that thing is. You want your current and potential customers to have an emotional connection to you, your company and your brand. They need to feel as though they are the most important thing to you and not their wallets.

10. Life learning

You're going to use social media to learn about your audience and you need to understand that this is an ongoing process. Who your audience is today may not be who they were 18 months ago or who they'll be in a year's time. Needs change, likes change, people grow and change. Social media is your inexpensive way to stay on top of and anticipate what your customers will need next.

You can use these changes to create and launch new products or services. Think about how compelling it is to the consumer that a new product was created just for them based on what they have said to you. Can you imagine anything more powerful than that? Nope, me neither!

Social media marketing strategies and tactics

After going through the process of laying out your social media marketing foundation and:

● Defining goals
● Evaluating resources
● Knowing where your audience is
● Determining what your audience wants/needs/likes
● Creating content
● Understanding how your marketing needs to integrate
● The 80/20 rule
● Quality over quantity
● Understanding who needs to control conversations
● Constantly learning about your customers

you now need to lay out the strategy or tactics that you want to use to reach your audience effectively.

We aren't going to go over every possible strategy for every possible social media tool. Each one could be a book in and of itself. What we are going to cover here are the basics. These are the building blocks to an effective strategy regardless of what tool you use to implement them.

Assess your environment

A situation analysis is probably one of, if not the, most critical components of any marketing plan. You want to take some time and gather information from a variety of sources including internal sources, newspapers, magazines, trade journals and other credible resources. The information you are gathering is really the '**You Are Here**' arrow on a map. You are going to see what is going on in your business and what is going on around you.

Some things you are going to look closely at:

● Product: what are you selling?
● Price: what are you charging for your products/services?
● Promotion: what are you doing right now to talk to your customer base and motivate them to open up their wallets?
● Place: where are you selling your products?

Once you have the answers for the internal items, move to external factors:

● Competition: who are they and what are they doing? Perhaps we need to define competition: we are going to go with the definition that your competition is any company that sells a product or service that solves the same customer problem that you do. Know what your competition is doing, what is working for them and what isn't and ultimately how you can do it better.
● Consumers: who is your market, where are they, what are they doing and where are they going to get their problems solved?
● Economy: this is fairly straightforward but just for fun this includes balance of trade, Gross Domestic Product (GDP) and consumer confidence.
● Regulations and laws: this includes what the Government has passed as well as regulatory agencies such as Financial Services Authority (UK), Environment Agency (UK), the Environmental Protection Agency (USA), the Food and Drug Administration (USA) and so on.
● Technology: this includes technologies used to do business and technologies used for suggesting new products.

Don't just brush over this. You really want this to be as detailed as possible because it is going to guide the decisions you make on how you are going to use social media tools to further your marketing efforts.

Know your audience

Notice how this keeps popping up? You have to know who you are catering to. Who is most likely to buy what you are selling? What is the best place to meet them and convince them you are the answer to their problem? It is your purpose to solve what ails them. If you don't know what's bothering them, or what it is they need you are going to have a problem reaching them.

Know yourself

You need to take an honest look at what your strengths are. For example if you are terrible at writing, the whole blog thing may not be the right tool for you. That is not to say that you can't or shouldn't blog, it means you need to find someone to convey your message for you.

What resources do you have that you can commit to social media marketing, this means money and products as well as time and connections?

Set goals and objectives

Create a set of realistic objectives you want your social media marketing to accomplish. You can do this with each tool. Say you are going to use Facebook: what is your goal? Do you want 100 likes in your first 30 days? Do you want to use Facebook as a customer service vehicle?

Set realistic goals: my recommendation is the usual 30 days, 90 days and 180 days until you get the entire first year. Take baby steps: you have to crawl before you walk, walk before you run. Social media marketing done in the wrong way is difficult to undo. Take the time to do it right the first time.

Keywords

Social media marketing is all about content. Quality content drives traffic. It gets the reader's attention and motivates them to take action. What is the most important part of quality content on the web? **Keywords.**

Search engine optimization (SEO) cannot be ignored in the realm of social media marketing. SEO, in simple terms, is the art of formatting your website's pages and your website as a whole so it shows up in the first page, or ideally No. 1, in the search engine results page for a given search phrase (which we call a **keyword**).

You can get an idea of what your target audience is looking for by going to Google and doing a search for 'Google Keyword Tool', then click the link to be taken to the tool.

I use this tool almost every day. To help find out what people are searching for, Google, in their infinite wisdom, have provided us with the means to actually see into people's minds, at least at the time they were searching for something.

Type in a keyword you think your customers are looking for (or enter your website address) and the Google tool will pop out all the related keywords plus how many times that phrase was searched for in the previous month and how much competition there is for the phrase in paid advertisements. (Only use the search volume numbers as a guide and for comparison purposes between groups of keywords.)

This initial research will help you generate ideas for content to bring people to your website or blog.

A bit of horrific but relevant self-promotion. If you're serious about your social media, you also need to know the basics of SEO. I highly recommend grabbing the companion guide to this book, *Teach Yourself Search Engine Optimization In A Week*. I also wrote it, so you know it's good!

Topics

You are going to get your topic ideas from your keywords and the knowledge you have about your target audience.

Your topics should cover questions that consumers have, give them information, entertain them and motivate them to want to come back.

Creation of content

The content you create should be on the planned topics you have. You can also share content that other writers have written. With that being said, you **must** credit your sources. You can use Google Alerts (http://www.google.com/alerts) to keep track of trending topics.

Top tip
Set up Google Alerts to send messages to your email every time there is new content posted about your keyword.

Top tip
Use Google Alerts to notify you every time a new mention of your company name is posted online. This will enable you to take action to fix a newly discovered problem or rectify a customer's bad experience almost instantly. Think that might look impressive to your online audience?

Social platforms

Look, there is no way to use every single social media platform out there. If you had a team of people dedicated solely to your social media marketing you might be able to come close.

The good news is that you don't need to use them all. You only need to use the social platforms that your audience is using. If it isn't Facebook, then don't waste time, energy or money on Facebook. Go where your potential consumers are.

Remember the Wikipedia list of social networking websites. Go back and read through them and also go to Google, Bing or whatever search engine you use and search for something like '[niche] social network'.

Engagement

Once you get the visitors, connections, likes and followers, what are you going to do with them? How do you plan on converting them from being visitors to customers?

Analytics

It's not a bad idea to measure the success of the social media platforms you are using. Understand that you don't want to dump a platform based on the first 30 days, but you do want to know if you should tweak what you are doing to get a better following and more interaction.

What aspects of your marketing do you need to test before you actually launch? Now depending on the size of your company and what it is you actually do, you may not be able to test a marketing message before running full throttle with it. If that is the case, start small. Don't blast every social media account you're planning to use, pick one, use it for 30 days, make some tweaks and then look at adding the next.

Budget

Before you cringe, generally speaking social media marketing is free. The cost has more to do with time than money spent. If you have to hire someone to manage your social media marketing, that is something else.

This is where we again want to point out that there is no such thing as a social media marketing guru or expert. There are a number of good social media marketing consultants out there and one or two excellent ones [ahem]. There are also people who specialize in a particular social media platform. For example, the way you use Facebook is different from the way you would use LinkedIn.

You also need to understand that they aren't going to do anything you can't do. You are paying them for their time and their expertise. Sometimes it is worth it, especially if you don't have the time to do social media marketing on your own.

Contingency planning

At some point, something will go wrong. What are you going to do? You need to have a plan because in the online world once something is out there, it is out there.

Fixing a failure as quickly and seamlessly as possible, so it doesn't have a lasting impact, is vital. Here are the main things you need to have a 'Plan B' for:

● Negative social media mentions
● Website downtime
● Product failures
● Unsatisfied customers
● Cover for illness or holidays

You need to be able to pay attention to what people are saying about you, your company and your products/services.

One person I know did a search every few days on Google for the company name and only what had been said about it in the amount of time since he last checked. (Alternatively you can use the Google Alerts hot tip no. 2 that I mentioned earlier to have these new updates automatically emailed to you or to the inbox of one of your employees.)

The no-nos of social media

We can also call this the 'What Not To Do If You Want To Be Truly Successful' and in honour and homage to 'the man', David Letterman, here are your top ten social media marketing no-nos:

10 **Don't break the golden rule:** be nice. Social media is very much a 'pay it forward' type of tool. Thank people and offer a helping hand.
 9 **Don't neglect your social accounts:** the last thing you want to do is create multiple social accounts and get bored with them and forget them, or worse, create only one that you never interact with. Be social and stay active to engage customers. You don't want to give a bad impression, as it takes too long to undo those. Would you open the doors of your store and then go for a walk leaving your store unmanned?

8 **Don't lie:** integrity is very important for the long-term success of your business. This is your reputation at stake here. Your avatar should be you, not someone else. Don't send private messages, tweets or updates that get people to click on a link that says something like 'click here to see how I got 10,000 FB likes'. Any links that you put in your updates should be to a blog post or article you have somewhere.

7 **No self-promoting and aggressive behaviour:** no, no and no again. Social media marketing is all about the soft sell. It is about building relationships. **Never** make your posts about selling a product or talk about how awesome your company is. Can you talk about a product or service? Yes, but make it about how that product or service can help your consumer. You don't even have to mention that it is something you offer. Look at the problem your consumers are having and offer a solution to them but don't 'hard sell', i.e. ask them to go to this link and 'buy today'.

6 **Don't create social media accounts without having the essentials in place:** you need to know who is in charge of maintaining and updating accounts, have a strategy in place **before** you start, and establish guidelines and a policy for your social media marketing.

5 **Don't apply a catch-all approach:** yes, naturally you would sell your product or service to anyone that came up and wanted it, but you can't market to everyone. Define your audience and go after those who are most likely to buy what you have to offer.

4 **Don't broadcast all the time:** people are following you for two reasons: they have a connection to your brand and you provide them with useful and engaging content. Don't inundate them with posts and Tweets. Then you become spam and no one pays attention to you.

3 **Don't remove issues immediately:** yes, you read that correctly. Don't take a negative comment or complaint down immediately on your Facebook page or wherever. Work it out, provide a solution. This shows consumers that you care and are willing to make an effort to rectify a problem. Only take it down if it can't be resolved.

2 **Don't have the personality of a wall:** your brand needs a voice, a consistent voice. You want to provide a familiar and comfortable atmosphere on your social media platforms to nurture and grow your communities. It doesn't matter if you have multiple people taking care of the social accounts; the voice needs to be the same.

1 **Don't ignore social media:** not too long ago, you weren't really in business if you didn't have a website. Now we have moved beyond that. To be competitive in this day and age you not only need that website but you need to be socially active. Consumers want to know the company they are considering spending money with. You need a social media presence to be successful.

Whew, that was a lot of information to cover in one day but I think you did just fine. In our next couple of chapters we are going to walk through getting you set up on some of the most popular social media platforms.

Summary

Tuesday was filled with creating your social media plan. This basically involved you determining why you are doing what you are doing by determining your goals and objectives to be able to track if you are achieving them or not.

Then you needed to determine *who* is doing the work of social media and *who* your audience is exactly. Then you determined *what* your quality content is, or at least you now have a good idea what makes great content.

You also know *when* you are going to have time and created a schedule to produce this great content. This process will never really end as you will constantly be learning and your audience's tastes will also be changing and evolving, so don't get complacent.

Lastly we determined *where* you are in the market. How do you compare in those categories listed to your competition?

SUNDAY
MONDAY
TUESDAY
WEDNESDAY
THURSDAY
FRIDAY
SATURDAY

This day then ended up with what to do when the you-know-what hits the fan, and the things you should never do on social media (be sure and write these next to your computer screen).

Fact-check (answers at the back)

Here are today's ten questions to help you remember:

1. Your different social accounts:
   a) Should each go in a slightly different direction to make sure all your bases are covered ❑
   b) Should all go in the same direction ❑
   c) Doesn't really matter which direction they are going, just need to be social ❑
   d) I pay people to think about those things ❑

2. You can have the best plan in the world:
   a) With the wrong people it can still succeed ❑
   b) With the wrong people it might do all right ❑
   c) With the wrong people it'll still be great ❑
   d) With the wrong people it will not work at all ❑

3. Knowing your audience is:
   a) Not necessary ❑
   b) Sorta necessary ❑
   c) Required ❑
   d) Not a good idea ❑

4. There are X number of social sites, where X means:
   a) 5 ❑
   b) 10 ❑
   c) 50 ❑
   d) Thousands ❑

5. What is better then having 10,000 followers that don't interact with your page?
   a) 20,000 followers that don't interact with you ❑
   b) 1,000 followers that follow your every post ❑
   c) Your dad as your only follower ❑
   d) 2,000 semi-interested people that are not your target market exactly ❑

6. You need to set what for your Facebook campaign?
   a) Goals ❑
   b) Objectives ❑
   c) Ideas ❑
   d) All of the above ❑

7. You should always have a contingency plan:
   a) True ❑
   b) False ❑
   c) It doesn't matter ❑
   d) It depends on the site ❑

8. Bad things to do include:
   a) Self-promotion ❑
   b) Aggressive behaviour ❑
   c) Not being nice and helping people out ❑
   d) All of the above ❑

9. Things to do include:
   a) Interacting with your customers ❑
   b) Being customer orientated ❑
   c) Always telling the truth ❑
   d) All of the above ❑

10. The worst thing you can do is:

a) Be a jerk ❑

b) Insult your customer's
   parents ❑

c) Ignore social media ❑

d) Be bland ❑

SUNDAY

MONDAY

TUESDAY

WEDNESDAY

THURSDAY

FRIDAY

SATURDAY

WEDNESDAY

Phase one of your social media takeover

Quick recap

At this point you should have:

- A clear understanding of what social media is.
- A better understanding of what social media marketing is.
- Good examples of how big and small companies have used social media marketing to improve their business in all areas.
- The basic principles that go into creating a social media marketing strategy.
- How to create a social media marketing campaign.
- What not to do in the realm of social media.

Today is a great day, because we are going to set up various social media accounts and finally get you all started. I will make sure you set these up the right way because it can affect all of your efforts from here on. (It is that important and I don't want you to knock it right out of the gate.)

Of course you can go back and fix things later, but doing it right the first time is easier than fixing it long after the fact, and if you do something wrong there is no guarantee you will find out about it anyway! (People *never* tell you why they don't buy.)

I want to make one thing clear: I cannot cover every single social media platform out there. Each could be a book all by itself so what I am going to do is break the 'Super Social 8' up into two days and teach you how to set up accounts on those platforms the right way the first time and the others that may be geared more towards your audience will most likely be similar.

Blogging

Before I dive into how to set up your blog, I want to provide you with a few statistics on why you should be blogging and give you some ideas on how to blog.

According to Mindjumpers:

- Blogs reach 80 per cent of all Internet users in the USA.
- Of all the time spent online, 23 per cent is spent on blogs (that is twice as much as time spent on gaming).

According to Marketing Charts:

- Around 60 per cent of bloggers post once a week, 10 per cent post daily.

There is a direct correlation between the frequency of blog posting and customer acquisition. Of companies that posted multiple times a week, 92 per cent acquired a customer through their blog. This is compared to bloggers that posted monthly whose customer acquisition dropped to 60 per cent and for those that posted less than monthly, their customer acquisition fell to just 43 per cent.

Blogs are considered the single most important inbound tool for marketing. They make up more than 80 per cent of the services that are used most often and are considered important or the most important tool for business. (Emphasis added by me.)

Blogs in general are free to set up and are usually part of the website you are creating or have. Writing the content of course is the tough part. If you don't want (or are not sure how to, don't have the time, etc.) to write the content, it is pretty easy to hire someone to do it for you and for a good price as well.

There are a number of great freelance sites you can turn to such as oDesk.com and eLance.com being two of the better-known ones. You can also run an ad on Craigslist (US) or Gumtree (UK) or even post an ad at your nearest college or university.

If you can afford it, find a professional consultant whose job is to create content that drives business, but if you're on a budget, I recommend hiring someone from either oDesk or eLance.

Note. Copy and paste any written content created for you into http://www.copyscape.com to make sure it hasn't been plagiarized from someone else before you post it on your blog.

Purpose of the blog

Blogs should be your company's online marketing nerve centre. They tie everything else together and are the next step to a customer making a purchase from you. If you have multiple social media accounts, then your blog should not be more than one click away from any of them.

Blog content makes a great thing to post and can get people talking. So regardless of which other social vehicles you use be sure to have a blog.

Step one: choose your blogging weapon

Now, let's get into what it takes to set up your blog the right way. We are going to start with the basics. The first thing you need to do is make sure you have a blogging platform installed on your website.

There are a number of different blog platforms out there and obviously I don't know where your website is hosted or what type of server it is sitting on, so you may need to confer with your geek-in-charge as to which blog platform is the most suitable.

One of the easiest to use (and my preferred blog system of choice) is WordPress, which can be downloaded free from http://www.wordpress.com. WordPress has made blogging a piece of cake. They have a plethora of widgets you can use and plugins you can get that give you more functionality and make optimizing the blog for the search engines a breeze. But to be fair there are other platforms such as Joomla, Drupal, Movable Type, BlogEngine.net and Expression Engine to name but a few. Do a little research at this point to find what will best suit your needs but always remember WordPress!

Step two: installing the blog on your site

Once you have picked the platform it is time to install it on your site. A lot of this will depend on the hosting service and the set-up you have running at this point. This could be as simple as running a script and then designating the directory you want the blog to be installed into. Assuming you don't have tech staff to do this for you, don't waste any of your own time trying to do this; you can hire a web developer from oDesk or eLance very cheaply to do this for you.

Step three: making the blog pretty

Design, while it might seem trivial, is something to spend some time thinking about. You should go with a design that is very similar to or the same as your business website. Fortunately there are thousands of free and low-cost customizable templates that make design pretty easy.

Typing something like 'free [blog system] themes designs templates' into a search engine should bring up all of the designs you'll need. One thing you should bear in mind is a lot of free templates and themes automatically add a text link back to the designer (or advertiser) at the bottom of each page.

My advice would be to spend a few pounds, dollars, etc. and buy a professional template or theme. For WordPress themes, I always come back to these sites as they all have plenty of choice.

- http://www.elegantthemes.com
- http://www.studiopress.com
- http://www.woothemes.com
- http://themeforest.net

Once you have the blog set up you need to think about the content. Take the time to research the keywords you should use based on your product or service and your customer base (use Google's keyword tool). You want to be sure that you and your customers are using the same language, otherwise they may never find you.

Your content also needs to be informative and engaging. This is the place for the soft sell. You don't use your blog to go 'This is my product/service, buy what I am selling now or else your hair will fall out and no one will like you.'

Instead you need to show them why they should buy from you. In the realm of types of content, there are three primary categories: newsworthy, evergreen and personal. Let's quickly go through those three, shall we?

Newsworthy content

Google released a new update in late 2011 that they termed the 'Freshness' update. The purpose of this update was to make it so that when certain queries are made, such as queries relating to major time-sensitive events, they are categorized differently and will rank better than other content written to meet traditional SEO strategies.

In other words, give Google what they want. Relevant, timely and engaging content related to high priority industry news. For example, if a new product or service is released in your industry or something is making news which you have expertise in, be sure and give the world your two cents on it and post it on your blog. You never know, one of your posts could suddenly get popular and go viral.

I remember reading a story about someone who wrote something on Michael Jackson a few hours before his death was announced. When he checked his stats the next day, he had thousands of new visitors and subscribers.

Evergreen content

This is content that you post that will forever be valuable to your readers. Say for example your business is in search engine optimization, the best tactics will change based on the new updates that major search engines make but the best practices will always be the same, so content talking about educating your customer will always be useful.

To get the most out of your evergreen content focus the content on good long tail keywords that are niche specific. These would be keywords that have consistently high search volume **and** a low number of competing pages.

Note. It is important that you focus on keywords that are specific to the niche you are working in because the search engines are getting smarter every day. If your site uses keywords with high search volumes that aren't specific to your niche just to grab traffic, you will be dinged and penalized.

Personal content

This is the content that you need to think of as you talking to your customer personally. This is where they get to 'meet' and get to know you, the proverbial 'person behind the curtain'.

This is very important content when you are thinking of social media marketing. It is also based on word-of-mouth marketing and relationship building. There is only so much that your customers need to know about you. They don't need to know what you had for dinner or if you painted your kitchen (I know it looks great but they really don't care), but they do need to know enough about you to learn to like you and also how your business came into being and the reasons why they should trust you.

Facebook

Let us start off again with a few statistics of businesses on Facebook to give you an idea about your competition.

According to Mindjumpers, practically every large charity and major university in the United States has a Facebook page, but less than 60 per cent of Fortune 500 businesses do.

Regarding wall posts on Facebook by your competitor's fans, 95 per cent are not answered by them! (What a great way to set yourself apart from everyone else: actually answer.)

According to Jeff Bullas, with regard to local businesses, 70 per cent already take advantage of Facebook (so this means your competitor down the road probably has a Facebook page). Good thing you have got me to talk you through how to run yours brilliantly!

Now for two **very important** stats about Facebook.

Facebook is the leading source of referred traffic at 26 per cent, compared to Twitter, which refers just under 4 per cent! This means if you're marketing to the general public and want to make real sales, go to Facebook (though Twitter does have its uses, which will be talked about later).

SMI has noted that 52 per cent of consumers no longer follow a brand on Facebook because the content that the brand posts has become boring and repetitive. (Don't make the same mistake.)

Now, if you are on Facebook for personal use, then you already know that it seems Facebook is always changing (err, wait, I mean 'improving') their service for users. So it should come as no surprise that they are frequently changing how businesses can set up Facebook pages.

As of right now, November 2012, this is the best way to set up your business Facebook page.

Classification

There are six different classifications you can pick from:

● Artist, band or public figure
● Local business or place
● Entertainment
● Company, organization or institution
● Brand or product
● Cause or community

The purpose of this classification is ranking: the more precise your classification, the better ranking you will get when users search. You also want to make sure you use relevant information to your field.

Basic information completion

Upload your photo. Facebook will prompt you to upload two photos: a profile pic and a cover pic. Facebook issues important guidelines for those pictures. One biggie is not to use your cover picture as an advertisement. What this means is that your cover pic can't just be made up of lots of words. It needs to be mostly just an image.

The profile pic is the one that will show up every time you comment on postings and is therefore really important. So this is the one image that everyone will see with everything you do on Facebook. Your profile pic dimensions need to be 180 × 180.

Then there's the 'About' section. This is a very short blurb, so make it concise and powerful as you only have two to three sentences. This will show up on your main page so make sure that it also includes a link to your website. It also needs to give the information that makes your brand different so that your page is more appealing to followers.

Admin panel

Consider this your HQ. It is from your admin panel that you want to manage your Facebook business page. The admin panel has a few options and features that you can use to optimize your page as well as get statistical feedback on your activity, so you will see how well posts are doing, which posts generate the most engagement and what went viral.

The 'Edit Page' option is in the upper right hand corner and it also has a number of options available. The first option is 'Update Info'. This tab will let you update your basic info. You can also fill in the form for the 'About' part of the Facebook business page that a follower can click on to read all about you.

You can also use the 'Build Audience' section to quickly and easily invite all of your friends to like your page and encourage them to share your page with their friends. To do this you need to fill your page with content. Once you get content up, take some time and invite some brand advocates to like your page. There are also Facebook advertising tools that you can use.

How to fill your page with content

The lovely timeline brought about the cover photo. Use this space as the 'stop, stare, I need to be there' image. You want that image to grab the audience's attention and make them read through your page. As we stated earlier there are requirements for the image. It needs to be 851 × 315 pixels. It needs to be mostly image. You cannot use it to run an advertisement. If you do, Facebook will shut you down.

Custom tabs

Facebook makes it easy for you to create an endless number of tabs on your page, but the four tabs that everyone sees first when they land on your page are the most valuable real estate on your page and are the only four that you can truly customize to fit you. What does this mean? It means that you really need to think about what you want those four tabs to be.

I recommend using a tab for your blog, a tab for your images, a tab for your videos on YouTube (if you have an account), and a tab for them to click that has a subscription form where they can give their email address for some cool freebie you will give away.

Posts

The content on your page needs to be a very nice mix of different types of content. Images, videos, music, polls, statements and so on. Knowing what your followers want to see and click on is important, so to start do a variety and then go back and compare them over the long haul to see which performed the best.

A new little useful tip for your posts

You can click on the little star in each post in your timeline to highlight the post horizontally across your page. Highlighting a post does two things. It makes it look like you have a cover photo in your timeline and marks the post as an event in your timeline. You want to highlight the posts that announce a new product, service or event. If you are in the business of promoting others, you can use the highlight feature to promote business associates, joint venture partners or other similar associates.

Monitor your page

Much like having a killer website is only great if people visit it, the same holds true for your Facebook page. Use the tools they give you to monitor what is happening on your page so that you know how to improve upon what you are doing. Learn the Admin panel inside and out.

Also, make sure that you respond to messages and posts that followers send to you. Keep the conversations going and set yourself apart from 95 per cent of all the other businesses!

Measure your efforts

By now you will have created and shared a business Facebook page, a page that accurately represents your brand. Now you need to measure all your hard work so you see what isn't working and how you can improve the Facebook experience for your followers and your business.

Remember social media marketing is all about relationships and word-of-mouth marketing. You want people to share your Facebook page.

It is important to say right now: it is possible for you to do everything right in terms of marketing and Facebook not be a success for you. Facebook does not work for every business.

Twitter

First, some stats. Mindjumpers states:

- There are over 140 million active Twitter users. (By active, we mean users who log in once a day.)
- One third of marketers have generated leads through Twitter and 20 per cent have closed deals.
- The vast majority (92 per cent) of retweets are on content that was deemed interesting.
- Almost half of all the Twitter users rarely post anything, instead they read and retweet the content created by others.
- More than half of the Twitter users access Twitter on their mobile device (keep this in mind).

Jeff Bullas shares:

- More than half of Twitter users use it to share new stories and links and the other half simply retweet.
- Of the 100 largest companies in the world, 77 of them maintain a Twitter account. Media outlets, however, are the most active users.

The set-up for Twitter is fairly easy and unlike Facebook, which is constantly making changes that most people do not want, Twitter is basically the same and has really only made minor tweaks for users to get the most out of their account since it started.

Jump on over to https://twitter.com and click on the 'create an account' option. All you have to do is enter your name, email and password. On the next screen you are going to be able to set your username (ideally this should be close to your business name) and once you submit that, your account is now live.

Twitter tries to help you find people, companies, charities and such like that you may want to follow with the Twitter wizard. They break it up so that you are following five in each category including, celebrities, businesses, technology, sports and other categories.

Make sure that you confirm your email address by clicking on the link that Twitter has sent to your email. Once you click on that link to confirm your account you can add more information about your business.

Go to the administration tab at the top of your profile. This is usually represented by a silhouette of a person or a cog, then click 'settings' and then 'profile'. Then upload an image. There are two ways to do this: use your logo or the image of the person who is going to maintain the account. If you use a person, remember that this person is going to be the face of your Twitter presence.

Enter your real name, insert your location, include a web address and write the bio about your business. This bio needs to include who you are, what you do and what you will be talking about on Twitter.

You can also change your design by going into the 'Design' area of your Twitter account. Here you can change the look of your Twitter page. Twitter offers a number of different set themes you can use or you can add a custom background image. There are also sites you can visit that offer Twitter 'skins' if you want to use them to help make your Twitter page stand out or you can hire a designer to create a custom one for you very cheaply.

You can also tell Twitter when you want to be notified via email. It can be every time someone mentions you in a tweet, when you get a direct message or if you get a new follower.

Twitter is where you are going to give short and sweet pieces of information that make your target audience do something. Either they visit your website, come into your place of business, follow you on another social site or go to another source to get more information. The goal of Twitter is to motivate your followers to do what you want.

For example, if you are a bricks and mortar business and you want them to come in, you can tweet a Twitter-only sale.

Super ninja tip
Google no longer indexes Twitter tweets in their search engine. Grab yourself a http://www.twylah.com account (currently free at the time of writing) and link it to your Twitter account. Each of your tweets will have a separate 'page' that is indexed by Google.

LinkedIn

If you are a company that caters to other businesses, LinkedIn is a social network that you **cannot** ignore. It is specifically for 'Business to Business' (B2B) companies.

Here is pretty much the only stat you need to know: it is the most effective social network for B2Bs with 65 per cent of companies on LinkedIn stating that they have acquired new customers through their connections on LinkedIn.

So we are going to jump right into the company set-up and we are going to operate here on the premise that you already have a personal LinkedIn account. (If you don't have one, you need one to do this and it is recommended you maintain both the company page and your personal page as well as it helps your customers feel they are talking with a real person.)

Log in to your personal LinkedIn account. On the homepage you are going to click on the 'Companies' tab across the top.

On the far right of the Companies page you will see a little link that says 'Add a Company', click on it. This will bring up a form where you will enter your company name and email. Once LinkedIn sends you a confirmation email you will click on that link to complete the building process.

Once confirmed, LinkedIn asks you one more time for you to log in to your personal account. This will then take you to your 'Company Overview' page. This is where you enter all the details about your company. Fortunately there is a LinkedIn page wizard that makes this a fairly painless process.

You can set up which employees (if any) will be admins on your company page. Should you choose to or be able to do this, those individuals must each have a personal LinkedIn account. You will naturally be the first administrator and the others below you. It is always a good idea to have more than one administrator just in case of an emergency, **but** make sure that the people you choose are people you can trust to represent your company.

Write your company description. This is the very first thing people will see when they come to your LinkedIn company page so **make it count!** This should be a concise explanation of who you are, what you do and why people should connect with you on LinkedIn. Remember this is a professional social network so this isn't where you are looking to make friends necessarily: you are looking to convey to other businesses why it is you they need to do business with.

Keep following the set-up wizard as it walks you through the setup-process. It is going to allow you to put in all the other places people can follow you or get more information about you.

Once all the information is complete you can start putting up status updates and building your following. Make sure to include your LinkedIn profile URL to your email signatures, website and all other online sources. This lets the people you already know, and who you are already connected with on other sites, to follow you on LinkedIn.

The best way to start getting leads is to go to the groups that are specific to your niche. Become active and post relevant questions and good info from your blog. Then, after a while of doing that, if you find a good opening or area that isn't covered yet, create your own group.

Summary

On this wonderful day we learned how to set up four different essential social accounts.

First, we set up your blog, which will become your nerve centre. Then, your Facebook account, where most of your customers probably are. After this your Twitter account; this is where you can drive traffic from. Finally we went through signing up for LinkedIn, the essential place to find B2B partners and other services you may need.

We went through the three forms of content that you should have on your blog: news-related posts (to show you keep up with your niche), evergreen content (solid principles that your readers will always find useful) and personal posts (that show your love for all things *Doctor Who*).

I also mentioned some things to get yourself noticed on these services, for instance the fact that 95 per cent of page posts by customers on business pages never get answered! If you can't run all these things yourself, in particular your blog, then I recommended looking into outsourcing to oDesk, eLance, or getting a consultant.

I told you about the ways to not get yourself in trouble on Facebook and get you the most business on LinkedIn. On Facebook be sure and don't put a call to action in your cover photo and on LinkedIn be sure to finish your profile completely and if possible get former customers to leave reviews or feedback.

Fact-check (answers at the back)

Ten questions for your faulty fuses:

1. Blogs are important because:
   a) They are the nerve centre for everything else ❏
   b) They are the next step on the purchase trail ❏
   c) They provide good content to post to other mediums ❏
   d) All of the above ❏

2. I recommend XXXX for content creation for your blog?
   a) A personal consultant ❏
   b) oDesk ❏
   c) eLance ❏
   d) Any of the above ❏

3. Which of these is not a form of content discussed?
   a) Newsworthy ❏
   b) Unique ❏
   c) Evergreen ❏
   d) Personal ❏

4. What percentage of business Facebook wall posts never get answered?
   a) 10 per cent ❏
   b) 30 per cent ❏
   c) 65 per cent ❏
   d) 95 per cent ❏

5. Posts should be:
   a) All of one kind (picture, video, or statement) ❏
   b) Diversified all the time ❏
   c) Diversified but with the type that tests the best as a slightly higher percentage ❏
   d) All one type per day ❏

6. It is always important to monitor what is going on with the Facebook page.
   a) True ❏
   b) False ❏

7. LinkedIn is best for B2B business, almost making it a requirement.
   a) True ❏
   b) False ❏

8. What percentage of companies that serve businesses on LinkedIn report making a sale simply through LinkedIn?
   a) 35 per cent ❏
   b) 65 per cent ❏
   c) 15 per cent ❏
   d) 96 per cent ❏

9. What is the most important part of the company page?
   a) The profile picture ❏
   b) The description ❏
   c) Your posts ❏
   d) All these and more are important because those who are searching for want a complete picture ❏

10. The best place to start getting contacts on LinkedIn is:
    a) Facebook ❏
    b) Chat rooms ❏
    c) The other niche specific groups in LinkedIn ❏
    d) Friends ❏

THURSDAY

Phase two of your social media takeover

Welcome to Thursday (yay, it's almost Friday!), where we are going to jump into the next four major social media marketing platforms. Can you believe that the week is almost over?

All right that is enough lolly-gagging, let's snap to it, soldier!

Quick recap

At this point, you should be familar with the following:

- What social media is.
- What social media marketing is.
- Examples of businesses big and small that have used social media marketing to improve all aspects of their business.
- The foundation of social media marketing and what it takes to create a social media marketing plan.
- How to create a social media marketing campaign.
- The things you should not do in social media.
- How to set up the first four of the big eight social media platforms: blogging, Facebook, Twitter, LinkedIn.

Today we're going to cover YouTube, Google+, Pinterest and StumbleUpon. Now, you're going to notice that I will be covering a couple of these four a little differently than yesterday. The reason is that Google+ and Pinterest are fairly new additions, not only to social media, but also to businesses to use for their marketing purposes.

YouTube

YouTube is an absolute must as part of your social media strategy. YouTube is now the world's second largest search engine (displacing Yahoo Search in 2011) and is, depending on who you believe, either the third or fourth most popular website on the entire Internet.

YouTube serves **4 billion** hours of videos every month and during 2011 had a **trillion** views (equating to 140 views for every single person on earth). People love watching videos and you need to figure out ways to exploit this incredible platform for your company or business.

YouTube has a Get Started page that walks you through the set-up process. You will want to think about the username you enter because it will become the name of your YouTube Channel. There are a few different ways that you can come up with your username.

The obvious first choice is to use your company name. That's great for companies that are already known. If you are a new start-up company with a strong brandable name, try and get it as your username or alternatively you can try to use your most desired keyword for the username.

Why would you do this? Google gives a little 'weight' to a webpage or URL when a keyword is in the domain name or somewhere in the URL (and if you are an SEO expert reading this and howling I'm talking rubbish after Google's Penguin and Panda updates, sorry, you're wrong).

When creating your YouTube username keep in mind that you can't have any spaces or special characters. You can however use upper and lower case letters.

Once you get all of that completed, YouTube is going to ask you to sign in with a Google account because Google owns YouTube. If you don't already have a Google account they are painless to set up and YouTube will offer you a link to set one up if you don't have one. I highly recommend you set up a Google account just for your business. You'll be using it for your Google+ account anyway!

Don't tie it to your personal account. In the world of business, keeping your business and personal activities separate is very important. Make sure you follow the steps to confirm your account. This is usually done with a confirmation text or email.

By now, you are a pro on setting up social media accounts. Setting up your YouTube account is very similar to the Facebook and Twitter accounts you already have. You are going to click the 'edit' button next to your profile section of your Channel. Make sure that you fill out every field that applies to your business. Keep in mind that the information that you put in here will help people find you. Tell them what they can expect from your YouTube Channel.

If you are a bricks and mortar business be sure to put in local information about your business.

Ignore the fields that ask for interest, about me, books and movies and the like if they don't apply to your business.

Customize

Above your channel are several buttons, one of which says settings. Click on that to create the right title for your company Channel and make sure to add tags to help people find your Channel. Click on the 'show advanced options' link to really customize the colour of your Channel and upload a background image.

Note. Once again, if you don't have the graphical skills or staff to do this, there are tons of freelance designers/artists who can do this for you cheaply.

If you use the modules, you can create different items that show up on your profile such as Friends, Recent Activity and Subscribers. Again, just as in Facebook when you are thinking about those tabs, think about what you want people to see right away on your profile.

Add videos

The whole point of having a YouTube Channel is to upload videos that help your brand. Let's say you don't currently have any videos of your own yet. You can look for other industry videos that are relevant to what you do and mark them as a favourite by clicking the 'add to' from the drop down menu under favourites.

Once you have a few, you can go to your Videos and Playlist setting and show your favourite videos as featured videos until you have created your own.

Promote your Channel

Just as with all other social media platforms, you are not the only user. YouTube has millions upon millions of channels. Your Channel needs to stand out in order to be found and seen. Add the YouTube icon to your website, take some time to browse other related channels and comment on their videos.

Using social media tools to promote your business is only one aspect of social media marketing: you will also need to promote the various other social media accounts you are using.

Major marketing trick alert. Where you can, embed your YouTube videos in your blogpost, Facebook pages and especially your Google+ page (discussed next). This is all tracked by Google, and they will give it a higher rank in YouTube (and ultimately Google's search index itself) the more you can share it and the more it is then shared after that.

Google+

According to MediaPost, the Google search engine is used by 85 per cent of the global Internet users on a monthly basis. Using that domination on the Internet in late 2011, Google launched Google+, their new addition to the social media landscape. Unsurprisingly, by September 2012 Google+ had more than 400 million registered users with 100 million active monthly users.

Even though only 25 per cent of Google+ users are deemed active, I personally believe that Google+ is the most under-appreciated social media platform out there at the moment and should be given top priority in your social media marketing strategy, regardless of whether you market to businesses or consumers (yes, even above Facebook).

Why? Two reasons:

● Google and Google+ are 'open' systems and networks. It's relatively easy to syndicate your content from Google+ to other places, including Facebook. It's extremely difficult to syndicate your content out of Facebook and Twitter.

- While it's true Facebook is the world's largest social network, Google+ directly ties into the world's largest search engine at Google HQ (**1.72 trillion** searches a year), which is increasingly using more social signals like AuthorRank to determine who and what should show in the top rankings for keyword searches.

First you will need to have set up a personal Google+ profile. Once you have a personal account you can begin setting up your business account.

Simply visit the 'Create a Page' on Google+ and follow the guided steps to get set up. You will need to pick from one of five categories:

Local Business or Place: this is any business or place that has a local address that customers can visit. If you pick this category Google will ask for your country and your phone number and if Google can locate you they will use the information they find tied to your phone number to populate your Google+ profile. If not, you can add it all in yourself.

Product or Brand: this could be cars, electronics, clothing and financial services to name but a few. With this option you simply enter your website and page name and pick the category that best fits your product or service.

Institution, Company or Organization: this category includes pages for non-profit organizations, companies and institutions. For this option you would list your page name and website and just as you would with product or brand, pick a category that most closely matches the type of company.

Arts, Entertainment or Sports: if you are creating a page about a movie, book or sports team this is the category you would pick. Here again you will need to enter your page name and website as well as choose the category that most closely represents what you fit into.

Other: if by chance you don't feel that your company really fits into any of the above categories this is the option you would choose. This will allow you to enter in your page name and website without having to narrow it down further.

All of the above categories require that you state whether your page's content is appropriate for users that are 18 years old and above or 21 years old and above and note if the content will specifically be alcohol related.

Customize

Do you notice a theme yet? It is important that you take the time to make your page on any social media platform noticeable because you are going to be competing against millions of others and you need to stand out.

Make sure that your profile includes a photo, your logo or the person that is the face of your business, or any other image that is relevant to what you do. Include your tagline. Once your customization is done, Google+ will ask you to share your page through your personal Google+ account. You can skip this step until you are completely done with your profile and have put content up.

Edit

This is where you are going to go through every possible item about your business and fill in the blanks for Google+. We mean from the name of your company to the description of your company to your hours of operation.

Include your website URL and all contact info such as phone, email, Skype, any other messenger service you use and so on. You can also include the links to your other social media profiles.

Adding Photostrip

Don't overlook this as it is an important part of your Google+ profile. These five photos will appear directly under your page's name and tagline. You can pick five photos that best represent your business or take one picture and creatively upload it in pieces (which can easily be done with Picasa, which is part of your Google account).

Your Google+ business profile is now complete and you are ready to start getting content up and engaging users.

Pinterest

On a personal level, this is a favourite! From a business perspective, if you can use Pinterest and use it correctly, you can beat every competitor you have because very few businesses are using Pinterest or taking advantage of the user base there yet.

So let's start with some interesting stats.

MediaPost states that 83 per cent of Pinterest users are female. In the United States the most popular categories are birthdays, fashion, desserts and clothes. Here is the really interesting information from MediaPost: 22 per cent of the 'pins' come from New York, 15 per cent come from Los Angeles and 10 per cent come from Minneapolis, which beats San Francisco with 8 per cent, even though Pinterest is based just down the road in Palo Alto.

Pooky Shares says that in the UK the most popular categories among users are blogging resources, venture capital, SEO/marketing, web analytics and crafts. Though Pinterest has barely been around for a year they tie with Twitter when it comes to the amount of traffic they refer to websites coming in at just under four per cent.

Not only that, but Pinterest drives more traffic than YouTube, Reddit, LinkedIn and Google+ combined and is becoming a leading driver of traffic to retailers. But it's not only retailers who can take advantage of Pinterest's incredible growth and engagement; service businesses can also leverage Pinterest.

One example is Mr Rooter, an American plumbing franchise who are using Pinterest to create top-of-mind awareness for their company by publishing funny pictures of their action figures in different locations around the world as well as creating a DIY board showing people how to fix simple plumbing problems around the home.

Now let's discuss the really interesting part about Pinterest and why you need to include it in your marketing plan. It is an image-based social network that grew an incredible 4,000 per cent during 2011 with more than 4 million users, hitting 10 million monthly unique visitors faster than any other standalone website in Internet history.

Not only that, Pinterest users only rival LinkedIn users for buying power!

So not only does Pinterest keep all of those users engaged, they also **buy!** The average Pinterest user spends an hour or more per month on the site. So Pinterest still has a lot to grow but when it does, if it continues to keep its users engaged, it will be massive for your business even if you're selling B2B.

Let's get set up

Originally you needed to be invited to join Pinterest, now you can simply sign up. You can create an account with your business Facebook account or your business Twitter account. After signing up you can create your username. I recommend that you use the same username here that you have on Twitter or Facebook because you want to promote brand consistency. Follow topics that are pertinent to your business and complete the process by following your Twitter and Facebook users.

Build your boards

The beauty of Pinterest is that as soon as you 'pin' something to your board it directs people to the URL that is associated with the image. So if you are a business that has products to sell, create boards around those products. But don't let your products be the only thing you pin about because that is going to turn your followers off.

Get creative

Looking at a bunch of boards all about products is boring. Create boards based around what your target audience is interested in. So let's say you have a clothing line, or fashion is your niche, you can create boards based on colours, styles, attitudes and accessories.

Interact

It is social, so it isn't just about your own boards. Take a look at what other people are pinning and comment on the images. You could even create a board dedicated to things that complement what you offer. Kind of a pay it forward approach, which can go a long way in attracting new customers and building relationships with other companies.

Google Analytics

Google Analytics will help you keep track of how many of your pins are sending traffic to your website. This will help you determine what pins your followers are responding to so that you can tweak your boards and create new ones based on engagement.

Just log into your Google Account and then go to http://www.google.com/analytics to get yourself a free account.

StumbleUpon

This is a bookmarking social media tool. So unlike everything we have talked about so far, you're not going to create an account and build a profile page and invite all your connections to come and follow or like you.

StumbleUpon is an excellent tool to have in your social media marketing plan because it isn't based on your network. Instead it will generate a larger number of random hits because StumbleUpon is open to a broader audience (over 25 million registered users as of November 2012 according to their homepage).

So now let's get you ready to take advantage of this service.

The set-up is really simple and self-explanatory. All you need to do is go to http://www.stumbleupon.com, follow the guidelines StumbleUpon has for small businesses and in a few minutes you will be up and running.

Next, you will want to allow discovery of your webpage. The beauty of StumbleUpon is users can select the type of content they're interested in, so by categorizing your content correctly you will get targeted visitors to your pages. When someone visits a page on your website, via StumbleUpon, a small banner will be floating at the top of the browser window where the visitor can then 'thumbs up' or 'thumbs down' your content depending on whether they like it or not.

The more times you get a 'thumbs up' the more your content will be shown to other people who have also mentioned they are interested in that type of content in their user profile. This gives your content the ability to go viral very quickly providing it's excellent.

You don't have to just rely on StumbleUpon users to 'thumbs up' your content. Each webpage you promote with StumbleUpon gets a unique shortened URL which you can send to other followers and subscribers on other social media platforms where you can reach out to them and get them to 'thumbs up' your content using the floating banner at the top.

Note. Make sure you are creating unique content for your web page. The better the content, the more visitors and 'thumbs ups' you are going to get. StumbleUpon also makes a point to highlight original work. This means that content that you simply copied and pasted from another source is not original or unique.

Summary

Thursday was all about signing up with four other social media spots, including YouTube, the giant of video that will drive lots of relevant traffic to your site. As well as that, getting a Google+ account is also pretty necessary as it has a lot to do with SEO and AuthorRank (be sure and check out the link to more info on that in the resources).

We also covered Pinterest, which is also a great place to reach women specifically (though more and more men are using it) visually, and the social tool StumbleUpon, which is great at broadening your base.

Be sure to put your keywords in your YouTube channel name if you can. Don't tie yourself to your personal account unless you want to make another personal account afterward. Be sure and keep things separate here (particularly with Google+ and YouTube pretty much auto-connecting now): be aware this can happen to you.

Some further tips: promoting your videos and all of your blog posts on Google+ will almost guarantee they will get indexed faster. Be sure to customize every page you

SUNDAY
MONDAY
TUESDAY
WEDNESDAY
THURSDAY
FRIDAY
SATURDAY

get your hands on, just remember to keep a common feel and logo through out. Every page should not be completely different.

Pinterest is great because you are probably already making images for Facebook, so why not post your images here as well? Remember to interact and post images from others as well as comment, and target your images at your general market and age.

StumbleUpon is a great tool to use to get traffic to your various properties, but don't just recommend your stuff. To use this right keep it open whenever you surf the web and be sure and highlight cool posts wherever you find them. This way, your posts of your content will never get flagged as spam.

Fact-check (answers at the back)

Top ten questions to keep this day in your memory bank:

1. YouTube is all about:
   a) Audio files ❏
   b) Videos ❏
   c) Music ❏
   d) All of the above to a greater and lesser extent ❏

2. YouTube likes it when you post their videos around your various other platforms (even their competitors as long as they get a link back).
   a) True ❏
   b) False ❏

3. Google+ is mostly populated by:
   a) Males ❏
   b) Females ❏
   c) Both ❏
   d) Unknown ❏

4. This is probably because:
   a) It makes business sense to be here ❏
   b) Men just are cool like that (oops did I give away the answer to the question...?) ❏
   c) They are experimenting ❏
   d) All of the above (though possibly not B) ❏

5. Pinterest is unique in that:
   a) It is all about images ❏
   b) It keeps its users engaged ❏
   c) Almost 25 per cent of its users are from NY ❏
   d) All of the above ❏

6. Pinterest is populated by mostly:
   a) Men ❏
   b) Women ❏
   c) Both ❏
   d) Unknown ❏

7. The best way to get followers is to:
   a) Interact ❏
   b) Interact a lot ❏
   c) Interact more than others ❏
   d) Interact only with people you like ❏

8. StumbleUpon is:
   a) A way to get your website in front of a broader audience ❏
   b) A rock you can trip on ❏
   c) A service which can drive lots of targeted traffic ❏
   d) Both A and C ❏

9. Who should you get to 'thumbs up' your content on StumbleUpon?:
   a) Anybody on StumbleUpon – it really doesn't matter ❏
   b) SU users who are interested in your type of content ❏
   c) Your subscribers and followers on your other social media accounts ❏
   d) Both B and C ❏

10. StumbleUpon could be the only source of traffic you need:
    a) True ❏
    b) False ❏

FRIDAY

Phase three: quality content creation

Alright, after today we only have one more day until you are ready to really get going on social media marketing. How time flies! Today we are talking in depth about content.

Content is the key to any marketing success and amazingly your greatest source of content topic ideas is your target audience. All you need to do is pay attention to what they are looking for and asking about and then deliver the content that meets their needs.

This is usually the part of marketing where we hear the biggest sigh, because writing is one of people's least favourite things to do. The good news is that you always have a few options when getting quality content created for your social media platforms.

Before we dive into your content creation options, let's do a very quick recap of what we have gone over to date.

Quick recap

- You know what social media is.
- You know what social media marketing is.
- We have gone over examples of how big and small businesses have used social media marketing successfully.
- You know what needs to go into a successful social media marketing campaign.
- You know the basic foundation that you need to have to build a social media marketing campaign.
- You know what not to do.
- You know the 'big eight' in the world of social media marketing and how to set up your accounts.

Content curation

The latest buzz in the marketing world when we are talking about creating good content is content curation. Unfortunately many businesses (big and small) don't understand what content curation is **or** how to use it to help with branding.

To help make this as easy as possible, let's define what content curation actually is.

Content curation is when a publisher collects the best content related to a very specific niche and targeted to a particular audience then embellishes that content through the addition of personal expertise and opinions. This embellished content provides increased value to that particular audience who reads it once it is published.

You may be sitting there wondering how content curation is different from any other form of content copying. The difference is that this content is:

- Editorially selected
- Provides added value
- Embellished

It is more than just regurgitating content that is already out there. The key is to retell the story with your personal slant to it. You must focus on the human element and always increase the value of what you are sharing in your content curation.

With that being said, let's take a look at how, based on a few of the social media platforms we have talked about, you can use content curation to your advantage.

Pinterest

The success of Pinterest in such a short amount of time is evidence that content curation works and that it is one of the hottest activities online right now. You should already have your account set up and we have already talked about creating boards.

Use Pinterest to tell the story of your brand to your followers. Don't just upload your own images; repin other user's pins so that your audience has a more cinematic experience with your brand. There is an old saying that a picture is worth a thousand words. Find those images that show your followers who your company is and what makes you stand out. Stick to these three principles:

1 **Authenticity:** you can't tell a story with images if you don't first have the story in words. Take the time to create your story. What brought your company into being?
2 **Consistency:** remember the human element (i.e. everything must be in order and make sense with your story) and the key difference between content curation and typical content aggregation (this is usually where a computer or a person who doesn't care just copies a bunch of slightly related material and puts it up hoping people find it). Make sure the images you use have a personal tie to your brand, your company's story and your personality.
3 **Fresh and pinnable content:** generally speaking, most brand engagement that takes place on Pinterest is tied to the company website. To encourage users to pin your content, add a Pinterest button to your website and a 'Pin It' button so that it is super easy for people to pin your content.

An online magazine

There are a few free content curation tools on the market that make it fairly easy to create your own online magazine that focuses on your niche or a topic of your choice. If you opt to do this, make sure that the content you are using is content that your audience is interested in. Remember they need to find value in the content or it isn't going to be read.

You can use paper.li, storify.com or scoop.it to make it simple to editorially pick content for your mag. Make sure that your content tells a story and gives your reader an 'experience'. Think about it like this. Disney created those attractions where you get to sit and watch a movie or a play and they make it 4D so that most of your your senses are engaged: sight, touch, sound, and smell. At the end of the day this is content curation as well.

While your content can't be scratch and sniff, it can be written well enough to make your reader feel like they are part of it.

Blog curation

One of the best examples of how to effectively use content curation on your blog is to take a look at what The Daily Beast (http://www.thedailybeast.com) does. They take some of the best content on the web and put it on their blog and allow writers to give their 'two cents' on the content. So it isn't that they are just keeping a log of comments at the end of the blog post, but writers take the content and interject their own thoughts and feelings into the piece.

You can also curate the content on your blog and then include individual posts throughout the day about that content. Each post that is added that day will provide additional commentary on the original piece, or you can give your readers an expert review/analysis of the content to add that extra value.

There are tools you can use that are free such as SocialMention (http://socialmention.com) or Google Alerts (http://google.com/alerts).

Email marketing curation

Creating an email newsletter is an easy and effective way to curate content and share useful information with your list. Here you can use content that you have already created for other reasons or you can use content that others have created.

Again, there are a number of really great tools that you can use to make the process easier. There is a tool that XYDO (http://xydocuration.com) offers that will help curate content for your email marketing and it gives the click-through rate a boost.

Top-quality content

Never compromise on quality. Often small businesses take shortcuts on marketing because they feel that once they have the flow going saving a bit of money or a couple of hours' worth of work won't affect profitability over the long haul. OK, the first time it may not, but the second and third time it is going to cost you customers.

How many times have you, or someone you know, said, 'Well so and so didn't use to do things this way' or 'I remember when I really enjoyed it here but now it just feels so blah'.

These are the feelings you generate when you deliver sub-par content and it will cost you customers. The content you put out should always be the very best you can do. When curating content is done, make sure that the original content is valid and that it matches your business and your brand. You may find it costs as much time to do that right as it does to come up with original content itself. Either way it is worth it.

Original content

I almost hate to even have to talk about why it is important to have original content, but just as social media has done wonders for connecting people everywhere it has a downside as well: content is copied and pasted and claimed as being the work of the person 'borrowing' it.

Nothing will cause me to immediately click off and ignore a website forever than when that website or company tries to use the work of someone else and claim it as their own.

Every second of every minute you have spent creating a killer social media marketing plan (or any marketing plan) will go down the drain the moment you start posting content that is duplicated from others. The search engines don't like it and will punish you severely for it and your customers won't like it either. The search engines will consider your site spam and your customers will consider you a fake.

It doesn't take much to write original content. Chances are pretty good that the business you are starting or running is a business that you are passionate about. Something made you start it, what was it?

Why is it an area you went into? Tell your customers why you started your business. Tell them why you are passionate about your service or your product. Tell them why they, the customer, matter to you.

You don't have to write a book a day. For most of the social media platforms we have talked about you only need a few sentences at a time to get a conversation going and have your followers respond.

If you really don't want to write the content yourself and you don't have a writer on staff, hire a freelance writer. You can find them on Craigslist, oDesk, eLance and a dozen other freelance websites. When you hire a writer there are a few things you want to look for and pay attention to:

Experience: they don't have to be professional writers for *The Times* or *The Washington Post*, but you do want to know they have written the type of content you are looking for before.

Native speakers: I am a firm believer in the fact that if you can't speak the language you can't write it convincingly, especially British and American English. Your writer needs to be able to speak to your audience convincingly to sell your brand.

Social media experience: we are talking about social media here, so I want to focus on looking for someone that understands how social media works because the content is a little different from basic web content. This content has to be monitored and responded to, and it **must** engage the reader.

It is up to you if you sign a contract with the writer or work through a service like the ones I mention above. You will want to proof the content and run it through copyscape.com because remember, in the end, it is your name and your company that is on that writing.

Another pet peeve of mine is reading poorly written content. It insults your readers and it tells them that you really don't care about them because if you can't take the time to write informative content that is written in the proper form, why would you care about an issue they may have with your product or service?

Top tip

To quickly double-check spellings and grammar before posting to your website, blog or social media account, copy and paste the content into Microsoft Word and hit F7 and Shift-F7.

Summary

Friday is here, and it was all about delivering great content to your subscribers via your blog, and Facebook posts, etc.

I described the latest fad (which is pretty cool and useful) called content curation. This is where you take other great content and inject a lot of yourself into it and embellish it a lot to make it almost a totally new piece of valuable content for your audience; this could be explaining a survey or simply explaining a really cool news item in your niche.

Pinterest shows us how content creation can work for images and videos. Definitely spend a bunch of time browsing through this place and thinking how you could do the same.

Tools for content curation include socialmention.com and Google alerts. Use them well and use them often! There are many uses for these two tools.

Nothing, and I mean nothing, really beats awesome quality original content that only you can create with your unique personality. Show your passion and zeal and let me tell you the search engines and people will find

SUNDAY

MONDAY

TUESDAY

WEDNESDAY

THURSDAY

FRIDAY

SATURDAY

you. It may take some time, but they will find you.

If you have to hire outside writers, be sure and follow the guidelines and be sure to check if it is fun, interesting and relevant before you post it, and never post something that you copy from someone else without acknowledging them as the original author.

Fact-check (answers at the back)

1. Content curation is:
   a) Copy and pasting content and having people comment on it ❏
   b) Editorially chosen, well embellished material that fits in with your brand where you acknowledge the original author ❏
   c) Content that has been gone through with a comb ❏
   d) What museums do ❏

2. The website that shows that content curation can work well is:
   a) Pinterest ❏
   b) Craigslist ❏
   c) oDesk ❏
   d) Facebook ❏

3. Another way to curate content and add value to it is:
   a) Create a website based on it ❏
   b) Make every page of your website about it ❏
   c) Create an online magazine ❏
   d) Phone a friend and tell them about it ❏

4. To see blog curation done well, go to:
   a) The Globe Weekly ❏
   b) The Star ❏
   c) The tabloids ❏
   d) The Daily Beast ❏

5. Email marketing curation is another nice way that customers would like to get content:
   a) True ❏
   b) False ❏

6. Your content should always be:
   a) Just enough to get by ❏
   b) Incredibly top notch all the time ❏
   c) Hit and miss ❏
   d) So-so (You are working on it, you can say...) ❏

7. A key to quality content is:
   a) Knowledge ❏
   b) Work ❏
   c) Passion ❏
   d) Intelligence ❏

8. Make sure if you hire writers that they have:
   a) Skills in your market's first language ❏
   b) Experience in writing about similar topics as your business ❏
   c) Experience in social media ❏
   d) All of the above ❏

9. A way to check content for duplication is:
   a) Copyscape ❏
   b) Spam Buster Plus ❏
   c) Google ❏
   d) Yahoo ❏

10. No matter what you do, do this:
    a) Try and trick your audience into buying ❏
    b) Create a good user experience ❏
    c) Enjoy yourself whether the audience enjoys it or not ❏
    d) Use others content and put your name on it ❏

SATURDAY

Managing, metrics and scaling up

Today I am going to just jump right into what you need to know and we will do a recap of the week at the end. There are quite a few things to cover and as we all know, time is precious at the weekend.

It is important to both monitor and measure your social media marketing efforts, but as with creating the marketing campaign, you also need to create a plan for measuring and monitoring.

Define your objective

In other words, why are you monitoring your efforts? There needs to be a very clear goal as to why you are putting in this extra effort.

Why will you monitor?

Here are a few possible objectives:

- I will monitor my social media marketing because I want to be alerted immediately when people are talking about me (negatively or positively).
- I will monitor because I want to be able to respond to my customers' questions/concerns quickly.
- I want to set up a system of information exchange with a support team so issues are handled seamlessly.
- I will monitor so I can join conversations quickly when people are talking about [keyword] so that I can enhance my credibility.

Where will you monitor?

Remember that we talked about social media being a two-way street? It is all about conversation. The heart of social media is to build relationships with your customers. But it is impossible to be on every social platform all the time or all at the same time... or is it?

There are fabulous tools like HootSuite or HubSpot that let you pull in all of your social networks and monitor and respond from one single dashboard. This allows you to see what is being said on your accounts at the same time and you can write a quick post and with a few clicks post new comments to one, two or all of your social networks at the same time.

Don't overuse this though because it shows up on your updates that you are using a service and some people don't like that because it looks like you just want to save time and not really spend time with them as a person (yes, it is silly but very real).

What will you monitor?

Monitoring is keyword based which means doing keyword research and choosing the right keywords is important.

There are the obvious words to monitor such as your name, the name of your company, your brand, your products and the names of other key players in your organization.

Prioritize your monitoring

There are just so many social media platforms on the web that you really don't need to monitor all of them. Decide what sources are most important to you and your customers and monitor those platforms. If you have a team, you can also monitor the platforms we will call fringe platforms (the ones where they may talk about you but not really where your target hangs out). A way to do this is just to use Google Alerts as we talked about earlier for picking up new content with your company name or about individuals in your organization.

Plan your monitoring

OK, so you are monitoring what people are saying about you, your company and your products. We all hope that it is all good that is being said, but what happens when there is a problem? How will you handle it effectively and in a timely manner? Remember that we said you don't always have to remove negative comments: they can offer the chance for you to show your customers your willingness to work things out. If you can't fix the issue, then remove the comments.

Sometimes you can't remove it though i.e. in the case of some of the local feedback. In this case, try and overwhelm the negative comments by emailing your list of customers and asking for positive reviews on the website that has a negative review.

Likewise, when people are saying good things about you, how do you show your appreciation?

Think about blogger feedback, customer advocacy programmes and possible joint ventures to improve branding for both partners. You need to think about all of the possible scenarios that social media marketing will open up to you and have a plan for handling them all appropriately.

Involvement of others

Let's face it, social media is a bigger, badder beast than anything else we have ever seen. Therein is the challenge. You may need a team to help you address the 'faster than the speed of light' tweet that just came out. How you handle this really depends on whether it is on you or if you have a team.

Frankly, I recommend pulling in at least one freelancer to help you stay on top of what is going on if you are a one-man/woman show. You really don't want to leave tweets, posts, updates, comments or feedback sitting there until next week. It is always best to respond within 24 hours.

Listen to your target audience

Hopefully in the course of your monitoring efforts you have come across one place that seems to be the place where you can get the most information about your industry or your target audience. Don't just create an account and start jumping into the conversation talking about your product.

Listen to what is going on, listen to what is being said, pay attention to the problem that is being talked about. Once you figure out the dialogue, the jargon they are using, the interaction among members, slowly start to get involved. Offer advice on how to solve a problem that you see people discussing. You need to establish yourself as someone who knows what they are talking about before you start pushing your products.

Inbound vs. outbound conversations

Outbound conversation refers to you proactively getting involved in conversations that are taking place out in the market place that focus on your area of expertise. Inbound refers to the conversations that people are having specifically with you.

When you are a part of a large discussion you don't want to put links to your website or your product demo. However, if someone approaches you directly it is acceptable to provide them with a demo or a link to your website. It is important to know the difference and pay attention to the rules of engagement for each type.

Relationship building

Once you have identified a few spheres of influence, it is time to look for ways to build relationships with those spheres. In any conversation that is taking place it is fairly easy to figure out who is driving the conversation.

Do not, however, just look at these thought leaders as nothing more than connections. You need to get to know them, understand where they are coming from and understand who they are before you make a pitch to them. One-night stands don't last for a reason. In the professional world you want to build relationships with those who have influence, that are going to last and that are mutually beneficial to both of you.

Tools of the trade

You need to select monitoring tools that fit/work with the social media platforms you are using. Make a list of what you need the monitoring tool to do and do the research to find the one that is going to work the way you need it to.

Taking it to the next level

Once you find what social media platforms work for you, it is time to take a look at how to expand. What can you do to pick it up a notch so that your social media presence is really on fire? That is really going to depend on the platforms you are using. I am going to list a few different platforms and provide you with three ways to ramp them up.

Blogs

Update your blog frequently! I recommend two to three times a week though other sources may tell you once a week. Just make sure it is more than once a month.

Post your blog post URL to your social profiles multiple times; use a tool like buffer.com that will post your link multiple times as it is fairly easy to have a post get buried by the stream.

Include social share icons at the top and bottom of your page. Why? Because some people like to share as soon as they land on your page while others share once they are done reading. Always make the share buttons easy to find and always encourage their use by mentioning them and even have pointing arrows at them if you can.

Facebook

Offer unique and free products available only to your Facebook followers. After all, who doesn't love free stuff, and you want to remind them that there is a reason to continue to follow you on Facebook.

Create a consistent visual brand on your page. You can customize your profile pic, your cover pic and the icons associated with the different apps on your page. Use them to reinforce who you are.

Encourage your fans to make sure they see your updates. Seems silly to even point it out, because if they aren't seeing your posts you may think this is a waste of time. However, due to the fact that Facebook is ever changing, just because someone liked your page in the past does not mean they are seeing every update you have. They need to follow these steps to make sure they see all of your posts (http://alwaysupward. com/blog/fb-fans-arent-seeing-your-posts-and-how-to-fix-it/).

Twitter

Make sure you have a username they will remember. Now it must meet Twitter character limits and be available, but you want a name that they will remember that represents your brand.

Split test your bio: routinely change your bio on Twitter and keep track of the number of new subscribers that you get with each bio. It can and will change!

Follow users that follow experts in your industry: do this to find new followers as well as to give your perceived authority a boost because what will happen is many of those people you start following will follow you back. Don't just follow though; also involve these leaders in your conversations and specifically tag them in some posts.

Google+

Take advantage of the enhanced video and image galleries: it is Google after all, and they do have the coolest media features out there so use them to your fullest advantage!

Post on a regular basis even if you are the only one doing it. Google+ will eventually explode due to the reasons I mentioned before. Don't stop or slow down just because you are the only one doing it. This is one place where being the pioneer in your industry will pay off.

Host Google+ Hangouts on air with YouTube; give your company's YouTube Channel a nice boost by creating a Google+ hangout with your followers and customers. Keep in mind that right now videos are ranking really well and take advantage of that.

LinkedIn

Make sure you pay close attention to the SEO keyword when you are working on your company profile. You want your profile to be available to those who are looking for companies or individuals with your expertise.

Join the LinkedIn groups that are pertinent to your niche. After all, how can you be an industry expert if you aren't engaged in groups that focus on what you do and interact with the people you want to connect with.

Start your own group if you can't find a group on LinkedIn that addresses your niche or your service/product.

Pinterest

Go after the micro-demographics. It is true that overall Pinterest is primarily populated by young to middle-aged females but you can look for subgroups within that demographic to appeal to. Like mothers who work from home and have small children or the twenty-somethings who are ready to get married for the first time.

Create themed boards based on industry trends. The board topics need to be narrow and monitoring industry trends offers you a great number of ideas to work with.

Take advantage of all three Pinterest linking channels: each pin offers you three chances to link the pin back to your website.

Summary

The last day of this week. Bittersweet. But today, we learned how to monitor and measure your social media program.

Be sure to define your reason for monitoring and what you are looking for. Then define where you are looking and use hootsuite. com or Hub Spot to really be able to see what is being said to you from everywhere you are involved from one screen.

Be sure to monitor at least your keywords, such as your name, the name of your company, your brand, your products and the names of other key players in your organization. Be sure and spend some time thinking on this section, as you might think of more.

After choosing where you will watch all the time, plan exactly what you will do when something bad happens. Will you personally get involved? Or do you have someone else that has a way with words that can do better?

Most of all, this day I hope you learn to really listen. Don't just sell all the time, but watch the conversations and the tones of them and

SUNDAY MONDAY TUESDAY WEDNESDAY THURSDAY FRIDAY SATURDAY

the questions being said and how they are answered, and so on. This way, when you start broadcasting and getting involved you will already have a good idea as to what is effective where you are.

Bookmark and highlight the things you learned in the 'taking it to the next level' section today. Get all your accounts up and running, start to get fans and content moving, then come back to revisit these now that you have experience: they will make so much more sense to you.

Fact-check (answers at the back)

Last set of ten questions for your brilliant brain:

1. First, you need to:
a) Get started monitoring ❑
b) Monitor for everything ❑
c) Check all of the social platforms at once ❑
d) Define what you are monitoring for ❑

2. Monitoring is:
a) Hard ❑
b) Easy ❑
c) Keyword based ❑
d) Needs to be focused ❑

3. If you can't remove bad feedback what do you do?
a) Give up and go home ❑
b) Find the person who made the comment and beg them to remove it ❑
c) Learn from it and move on ❑
d) Overwhelm it by emailing your happy list of customers ❑

4. It is probably not good:
a) To go it alone ❑
b) To try and do everything yourself ❑
c) To not have a team ❑
d) All of the above ❑

5. Hootsuite:
a) Helps with searching Google ❑
b) Keeps track of all your social accounts ❑
c) Responds to all your accounts ❑
d) Both B and C ❑

6. When dealing with other leaders in your industry:
a) You should ask to partner with them first thing ❑
b) Learn as much about them as possible before approaching them ❑
c) Keep sending them messages until they respond ❑
d) Just friend them and wait for them to contact you ❑

7. You should blog:
a) As much as possible ❑
b) Once a month ❑
c) Four times a month ❑
d) At least two or three times a week ideally ❑

8. You need to treat your Facebook followers:
a) The same as everyone else ❑
b) Specially: you should give them special sales/services to make it worth following you there ❑
c) Worse than the rest ❑
d) Indifferently: you need to just post stuff through Hootsuite not directly interact with them. ❑

9. LinkedIn profiles should be keyword-rich so it is easier for your potential clients to find you.
a) True ❑
b) False ❑

10. On Pinterest you should going for:

a) The masses ❏
b) The individual ❏
c) Men ❏
d) Micro-markets of the female gender ❏

SUNDAY MONDAY TUESDAY WEDNESDAY THURSDAY FRIDAY SATURDAY

Surviving in tough times

I know times are difficult and there is a lot of uncertainty out there. So with that in mind, I've put together 10 tips below specifically for breaking through during these times of economic stress (potentially for you and your potential customers). Because remember, they have it rough as well!

1 Follow your passion

Regardless of the big picture economic situation there will always be potential clients and customers out there for your passion. Why? Say you have a passion for pickles. You just really like how they taste so much that you can't go a month without trying a new one. Say 1 per cent of the population of the US loves pickles and would probably like a pickle of the month service. That gives you 3,060,000 prospects! Think you could find 1,000 people that you could make $10 a month off of? Yes you could and that is regardless of the economy. But it would have to be your passion; it doesn't work if you aren't having fun.

2 Take full advantage of free/low cost tools

There were many tools listed in this book that had little or no cost associated with them. Be sure to use them! Don't just assume that paid means better or that you really can't start without a lot of money. That is simply not true. The main cost of 'social media' is time, which brings me to my next point.

3 Use your time wisely

You may be stressed and working 3 part time jobs right now to make ends meet. Don't let this stop you from following your social goals. Find just 1-2 hours a day to yourself, and use it for your business. Hootsuite will even let you schedule your tweets and posts so if this time is late at night then just schedule your posts for when people are awake.

4 Post on your lunch break

On your lunch break (Or any free time really) take 10 minutes to surf for a cool picture and post it with a call to action to Facebook or Pinterest and then deal with any fan posts or tweets. Make a habit of it by telling yourself that you can't eat or do something else that you would rather do until you do that first. Even a low-end cheaper smartphone will let you do all this.

5 Start with just a blog and Facebook

If your time and finances are very stretched, and I had one thing I could tell you to do, it would be to start a free blog on WordPress or Blogspot (owned by Google), hook these to a Tumblr page and then start a Facebook page. You can add in a payment page via Paypal or Gumroad and simply blog on your passion (With a mind towards keywords gained from the Adwords keyword tool). This covers the major points and can start gaining you an audience slowly but surely. As time goes on you can add further avenues.

6 Always respond to everything

Just like if someone tags you in a post you are almost obligated to say something. Make sure you are responding to every message, post, tweet and comment with something with 24 hours (The sooner the better though). If it is only a quick (and uniquely written; see next tip) 'Thanks for the great comment!' then at least it shows people you are reading the post and are interested in interacting with them. Otherwise they will consider you just another of the 95 per cent of businesses that never really show they care.

7 Be real

Don't end up sounding like a robot online to your customers by using cut and paste responses. If you do hire someone from out of the country to do your posting, make sure they understand this. Write with a real 'feel' to your words. You know instinctively when this happens to you, so don't treat your customers the same; be real.

8 Respond well to criticism

Say you don't make a shipment on time and someone goes on your Facebook and posts, 'Hey, where is my package, you bum?' Don't respond with silence or just remove the post. Use the chance to respond graciously with real understanding and tell them what happened. Maybe you got sick or it looks like the courier mis-delivered the package.

9 Don't get distracted

As you go along on your online journey you will run across many that have different ways of doing things or the latest greatest app. Whatever it is, don't just go after it: keep doing what you are doing and then incorporate it if you want. Don't let it distract you from actually doing something on your site. For instance you can find a webinar for pretty much every day in the week that will give you free tips on Facebook. If all you do is watch webinars though, who will post on your page?

10 Keep going

This was not a get rich quick guide for a reason. Anything worth doing takes time and work. If you work at it and keep going with your passion it will lead to opportunities you never dreamed of. So keep going and have fun!

Answers

Sunday	Wednesday	Saturday
1. D	1. D	1. D
2. D	2. D	2. C
3. A	3. B	3. D
4. B	4. D	4. D
5. D	5. C	5. D
6. C	6. A	6. B
7. D	7. A	7. D
8. A	8. B	8. B
9. A	9. D	9. A
10. C	10. C	10. D

Monday	Thursday
1. C	1. D
2. D	2. A
3. B	3. A
4. B	4. D
5. A	5. D
6. B	6. B
7. D	7. B
8. D	8. D
9. B	9. D
10. D	10. B

Tuesday	Friday
1. B	1. B
2. D	2. A
3. C	3. C
4. D	4. D
5. B	5. A
6. D	6. B
7. A	7. C
8. D	8. D
9. D	9. A
10. C	10. B

Notes

ALSO AVAILABLE IN THE 'IN A WEEK' SERIES

BODY LANGUAGE FOR MANAGEMENT • BOOKKEEPING AND ACCOUNTING • CUSTOMER CARE • DEALING WITH DIFFICULT PEOPLE • EMOTIONAL INTELLIGENCE • FINANCE FOR NON-FINANCIAL MANAGERS • INTRODUCING MANAGEMENT • MANAGING YOUR BOSS • MARKET RESEARCH • NEURO-LINGUISTIC PROGRAMMING • OUTSTANDING CREATIVITY • PLANNING YOUR CAREER • SPEED READING • SUCCEEDING AT INTERVIEWS • SUCCESSFUL APPRAISALS • SUCCESSFUL ASSERTIVENESS • SUCCESSFUL BUSINESS PLANS • SUCCESSFUL CHANGE MANAGEMENT • SUCCESSFUL COACHING • SUCCESSFUL COPYWRITING • SUCCESSFUL CVS • SUCCESSFUL INTERVIEWING

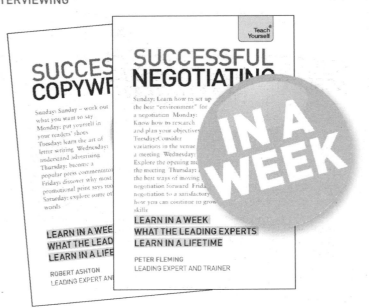

For information about other titles in the series, please visit
www.inaweek.co.uk

ALSO AVAILABLE IN THE 'IN A WEEK' SERIES

SUCCESSFUL JOB APPLICATIONS • SUCCESSFUL JOB HUNTING
• SUCCESSFUL KEY ACCOUNT MANAGEMENT • SUCCESSFUL LEADERSHIP
• SUCCESSFUL MARKETING • SUCCESSFUL MARKETING PLANS
• SUCCESSFUL MEETINGS • SUCCESSFUL MEMORY TECHNIQUES
• SUCCESSFUL MENTORING • SUCCESSFUL NEGOTIATING • SUCCESSFUL
NETWORKING • SUCCESSFUL PEOPLE SKILLS • SUCCESSFUL
PRESENTING • SUCCESSFUL PROJECT MANAGEMENT • SUCCESSFUL
PSYCHOMETRIC TESTING • SUCCESSFUL PUBLIC RELATIONS •
SUCCESSFUL RECRUITMENT • SUCCESSFUL SELLING • SUCCESSFUL
STRATEGY • SUCCESSFUL TIME MANAGEMENT • TACKLING INTERVIEW
QUESTIONS

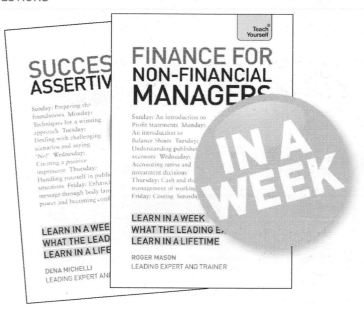

For information about other titles in the series, please visit www.inaweek.co.uk

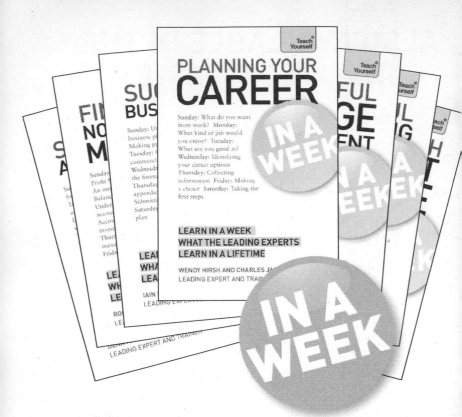